MILITA
OF WES

GW00361520

Paul Jackson

ACKNOWLEDGEMENTS

Grateful thanks are extended to Mike Bursell, who contributed much to the preparation of this book. 'Mr Huey' was a valued collaborator, whilst additional data was generously provided by Peter Foster, Tony Kearns and Lindsay Peacock.

Four squadrons of RAF Tornado GR1s, including No 17, remain based in Germany. Their base at Brüggen is surrounded by forest. *RAF/Sgt Rick Brewell*

First published 1994

ISBN 0 7110 2247 X

Published by Ian Allan Publishing

an imprint of Ian Allan Ltd, Terminal House, Station Approach, Shepperton, Surrey TW17 8AS; and printed by Ian Allan Printing Ltd, Coombelands House, Coombelands Lane, Addlestone, Weybridge, Surrey KT15 1HY.

CONTENTS

1. INTRODUCTION

Following from the success of *abc UK Military Airfields* (published by Ian Allan Ltd in 1992), this book takes the more adventurous military aircraft enthusiast across — or now, indeed, *under* — the Channel to western Europe. Here exist in quantity the aircraft which are seen in small numbers visiting UK air bases as well as those which have little or no business on Britain's shore and must be sought out in their native habitat if they are to be recorded in notebook and on film.

In addition to logging and 'photogging', the serious enthusiast will give some consideration to the history and geography of the air bases he or she visits. Stations in the UK have interesting stories to tell; abroad the diversity is far greater. Open days will give the opportunity to enter the base and study its residents and infrastructure in detail. For the remainder of the year, outside observation is all that is possible — sometimes.

Opponents of closer ties between the UK and Europe have cited the all-pervading influence of the European Commission which allegedly standardises everything from the length of the working week to the permitted curvature of cucumbers. Such is most definitely not the case with regard to the attitude of military police to aircraft enthusiasts. This varies from country to country and even between bases. Those used to the conventions of aircraft spotting in the UK would be most unwise to assume the same ground rules apply even within EC countries.

None of the nations covered by this volume has recently committed a spotter to a long prison sentence. However, some enthusiasts have returned from their travels minus film and, in extreme cases, lacking their cameras. It is to be hoped that, in the long term, the end of the Cold War will bring increased tolerance of those whose wont it is to lurk outside military establishments.

Meanwhile, circumspection is advised, even when on the balconies of civilian air terminals which exist at some otherwise military airfields. If there are local enthusiasts around, it is instructive to observe what they do — and, more importantly, what they do not do. Most will be happy to explain the local 'rules of the game' to a foreign visitor.

The best views of some airfields are obtained from land which is off obviously public roads and may be private property. This author has neither the time nor inclination to qualify as an international lawyer specialising in citizen's rights and the diverse rules of trespass in 10 countries. Suffice it to say, therefore, that extreme respect for property and politeness to local inhabitants ensures a low profile. That, in turn, can greatly reduce the possibility of a compelling invitation from the base's chief security officer. The following simple rules should be obeyed:

- Park vehicles in a safe position where they will not cause an obstruction on public or private property.
- Keep to established paths and tracks; do not damage crops or hedges; do not disturb livestock.
- Do not enter military property or damage fences; keep vehicles away from crash-exits.
- If in doubt, don't.

2. COUNTRIES COVERED

This book has been prepared for the benefit of enthusiasts making a medium-range foray into the European continent or travelling in the opposite direction to the Republic of Ireland. Its main area of coverage is therefore from the Jutland peninsula to the Iberian peninsula, progressing as far east as Austria.

Within this area are some 230 active military air bases operated by local air forces, armies and navies as well as overseas stations of the USA and UK. Detailed coverage of all of these would be impossible within the confines of a pocket-book, so it has been necessary to limit the number receiving comprehensive treatment to 68. However, the location and resident units and aircraft of the remainder are included for completeness, as are similar details of some 40 airfields closed since the end of the Cold War. NATO reserve airfields find brief mention for no better reason than that they are largely forgotten, but the line has been drawn at

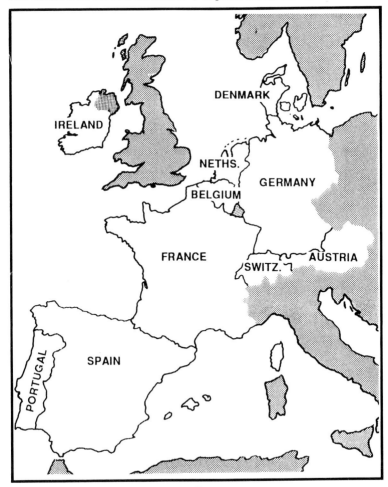

occasionally-used helicopter landing pads at military camps.

Maps and histories are provided for bases likely to attract the most interest. These are airfields housing fast jets or large maritime and transport aircraft. Some which are more civilian than military are omitted — such as Melsbroek, Belgium, which is part of Brussels International Airport. In the other direction, self-imposed rules have been broken to include the French maintenance unit at Châteaudun, which is popular with enthusiasts in spite of being a non-operational station.

Bases operating helicopters are banished to the 'Other military air bases' sections of this book, but not because of any conscious policy of ignoring army aviation and some aspects of naval flying. As noted above, helicopter airfields, plus those of training units, are included in the maps which begin each national section so that readers planning a travelling holiday can determine the most promising route.

3. INFRASTRUCTURE AND DEVELOPMENT

Many factors have shaped military air bases in western Europe, the most significant of which have been the formation of NATO and the 1967 Six Day War between Israel and its neighbours. Established airfields in Denmark, Benelux and France suffered considerably during World War 2, typically being bombed by Germany in 1940; built-up in 1940-41 for operations against the UK; bombed by the Allies in 1944; and renovated by their original operators — or, in Germany, the occupying powers — from 1945 onwards. Most permanent bases had, by then, gained concrete runways, and from these were operated the first jet fighters.

Although initiated in 1948, NATO did not have a significant impact on western Europe until after the Korean War began in June 1950. Concerned that this might be the prelude to an attack on the European democracies, NATO began a programme of air base construction to accommodate a build-up of local air force strengths and an increase in the size of US forces in Europe. The occupying forces in Germany realised that a sudden Soviet attack would swamp many of their bases, so new installations were constructed as far to the west as possible. Brüggen, Geilenkirchen and Laarbruch were built for the RAF within yards of the Netherlands border, whilst the US Zone housed others a few miles from the French border.

Until the French withdrawal from NATO in 1966, northeastern France was home to US and Canadian aircraft, whilst fighters of the *Armée de l'Air* flew from runways in Germany. From 1956 onwards, West Germany began re-forming its flying services and taking over some of the vacated bases closer to the border with East Germany. Fritzlar, for example, once a prominent *Luftwaffe* night-fighter station, passed to the RAF in 1945 and is now a base for German army helicopters.

The new bases which appeared like a rash over western Europe during the mid-1950s emphasised the meaning of the expression, 'NATO standard'. Built for the jet era, they normally comprised a single runway and at least one parallel taxiway. Even when existing airfields were upgraded, few attempts were made to offer alternative directions when the main runway was subjected to crosswinds. Many German runways fall between 7,995 and 8,012ft, whilst 2,400m (7,874m) appears with great regularity on French airfield maps.

Outside the expected main area of East-West conflict, airfields in Spain and Portugal developed at a less intense rate. Spain, though not a NATO member, signed a defence agreement with the USA in 1953 which brought American military bases and corresponding infrastructure. Morón, Torrejón and Zaragoza became bases for regular Strategic Air Command deployments and Rota was constructed for the US Navy. Spain's reward was in military technology, and the licence-built German aircraft which predominated in the front line were gradually replaced by jet fighters requiring hard runways.

Not all the airfields built in the 1950s were used to their full extent. NATO planning included reserve runways, to which were later added other stations as force levels reduced. When planning changed to include provision for tactical reinforcements from the USA during a European conflict, the spare bases were earmarked for units which would transit the Atlantic to bolster the front line.

Weelde in Belgium and de Peel, Netherlands, are but two installations where minimal regular activity conceals a greater purpose. Vandel, Denmark, is a permanent station whose resident army aircraft could operate from a football pitch but which have a 9,000ft runway and acres of hardstandings at their disposal. French bases were lost to NATO after 1966 and some never housed military aircraft again. Grostenquin (Canada) and Chaumont, Dreux and Laon (all USAF) all became derelict in this way.

The two central European neutrals were not always thus. Austria, a former ally of Germany, was occupied until 1955, then granted autonomy on condition that non-offensive armed forces were maintained. The air force and its infrastructure reflect low budgets and a front line which is one or two combat aircraft generations behind the major powers. Switzerland, by contrast, invests heavily in defence of its neutrality. With flat land at a premium, airfields are squeezed between villages and not infrequently are traversed by public roads. In addition to the regularly-used bases, there is a further network of wartime airstrips, both making use of underground hangars for additional security from attack.

As such, Swiss thinking was ahead of NATO until Israel's lightning decimation of its opponents' air forces in June 1967. Lines of parked Arab aircraft were destroyed by pre-emptive attack at the very time that NATO was reconsidering its 'tripwire' policy of all-out nuclear response to aggression. The new doctrine of 'flexible' response — a reaction in equal measure to any Warsaw Pact move — might require air operations over days or weeks, during which time aircraft would have to be protected against raids.

Accordingly, the 1970s was the decade of the hardened aircraft shelter (HAS). Several designs of HAS appeared on both sides of the central German border, but each had core elements of a curved roof with reinforced doors at one end and hot gas outlet at the other. Those constructed in France and East Germany tended to be simplest and smallest, sometimes (initially in France) lacking the protection of a door.

The later NATO HAS designs added an annexe for equipment storage to improve autonomous operation and some early constructions were similarly upgraded, notably in RAF Germany. Three main types of door design include the earliest system of two hinged, clam-shaped doors opening under an extension to the roof; and the more recent system of flat doors moving on wheels at right-angles to the HAS centreline. In Denmark will be found a third type in which a single-piece door turns through 90° to lie flat in a ground recess and becomes part of the HAS floor.

Accompanying the HAS were associated programmes to tone down aerodrome buildings and improve ground defences against attacks by Spetsnaz troops. Building of 'HAS farms' increased the area to be defended and sometimes involved purchase of additional farmland to extend the base. More recently, the USAF, at least, has seen the futility of trying to hide sprawling airfields in the age of the INS and GPS and has painted some of its bases in brighter colours. The HAS policy now extends into Iberia, hiding most fighter and interdictor aircraft from the enthusiast's gaze until they are ready to fly.

At some bases, aircraft have not been easy to see at the best of times. Germany, in particular, appears to have a preference for building airfields in forests and/or relying on trees within the boundary to give seclusion to parking areas. Road-signs to air bases are far less conspicuous than would be expected by the British visitor, thereby demanding greater map-reading skills from the itinerant enthusiast.

4. HOW TO USE THIS BOOK

For ease of reference, air bases are covered under national headings, listed alphabetically from Austria to Switzerland. Within each national chapter, principal airfields are also covered in alphabetical order, those of lesser importance relegated to a simple listing at the end of the section. It is not unusual for bases to have alternative names, but the full titles will be found on the map which accompanies the introduction to each national section.

Fast jet, maritime patrol and most transport bases are covered by a map and a short history which includes mention of the currently based units and their aircraft. Maps are to the scale of 1in to 1 mile, except that widths of roads and runways have been exaggerated for clarity. Lengths are proportional and all maps are orientated 'north up'.

In most cases, it has been possible to show taxiways as an aid to determining the best position (if any) for ground photography. Position of trees has been difficult to establish with accuracy, but known woods are shown as shading. Many more obstacles exist to frustrate the enthusiast. In all except a few instances — in which maps would have to be inordinately large — the roads which encircle an airfield are shown, indicating at a glance how the perimeter may be traversed.

A good road map will still be required for planning a visit abroad. Most of Europe is available in 150,000 to 200,000 scale at reasonable cost — ie, around £12-15 for the whole of France or Germany. Michelin maps of France, Belgium and some other countries are the most useful, as every small flying club airfield and upwards is distinctly shown. On the other hand, maps of Germany deliberately omit all traces of air bases — even when an 8,000ft strip of white in the centre of a green forest is rather a give-away! Similar problems obtain in Switzerland. For this reason, the location of all minor airfields mentioned in this book is given as a distance and bearing from significant habitation.

Roads and tracks which appear on the sketch-maps in this volume are believed to be public property and are depicted as such in good faith. The author and publisher accept no responsibility for the consequences of errors. Road numbers are included where they exist, but many are unclassified. Railways and watercourses are shown, as they normally present an obstacle to cross-country progress.

Enthusiasts touring the continent will try to time their visit so that they may take in air shows and squadron exchanges/NATO exercises. Details of the former appear in many aviation magazines; advance notification of the latter is restricted to private-circulation publications for the dedicated enthusiast.

Only in a few cases has mention been made of preserved aircraft forming a museum at, or close to, an air base. Travellers not in a tearing hurry will wish to make minor detours from their route to see other interesting machines. Essential companions for this are *European Wrecks & Relics* by Mike Bursell and volumes 3 and 4 from the series 'Aircraft Museums and Collections of the World' by Bob Ogden.

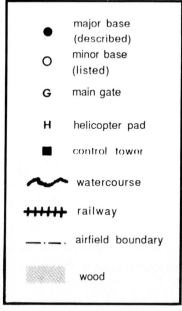

●	major base (described)
○	minor base (listed)
G	main gate
H	helicopter pad
■	control tower
〰	watercourse
┼┼┼┼┼	railway
─ · ─ ·	airfield boundary
▨	wood

SCALE

⊢━━━━━┥

1 mile

AUSTRIA

Austria's small air force, the *Osterreichische Luftstreitkräfte*, is charged with defending the neutrality of this German-speaking, Alpine republic under the terms of the 1955 State Treaty. The Treaty allowed Austria independence in return for certain limitations which, in the case of the OLk, included a ban on the use of guided missiles. In fact, financial restrictions have been more effective in keeping the OLk as a non-aggressive force, but the 'missile ban' — intended more to cover V-1 and V-2 types of weapon then SAMs and AAMs — has weakened air defence for more than two decades. Only with the 1988 delivery of ex-Swedish SAAB Drakens was Austria allowed to obtain missile armament (AIM-9 Sidewinders) for its interceptor force.

Austria formed an air section of its Defence Bureau on 13 September 1955 and two months later the government assigned it the airfields at Aigen-im-Ennstal, Hörsching, Tulln/Langenlebarn, Wiener-Neustadt and Zeltweg. Of these, Langenlebarn was chosen as the first to house active units and it was from here on 9 December 1955, PolObstlt Gustav Hauck took off in Yak-18 3A-AB to fly the first sortie of the reborn Austrian Air Force. Four Yak-11s and four Yak-18s were amongst the initial equipment of an air arm intended to expand to 335 aircraft, including 174 fighter-bombers and 57 reconnaissance machines. However, the government hesitated to accept aircraft offered by NATO and the target strength was revised smartly downwards. Not until 1961 were jet fighters obtained when Sweden offered 15 obsolescent SAAB J-29Fs, which were joined by a further 15 two years later.

In July 1967, the Defence Council decided to order the even less suitable SAAB 105Oe as Austria's new combat aircraft. Two interceptor and two fighter-bomber squadrons shared 40 aircraft and only with the arrival of Drakens did the interceptor arm gain its first radar-equipped aircraft. Today, the OLk is largely equipped with STOL light aircraft and helicopters which are suitable for army support and SAR in mountainous terrain. Helicopters are based at Langenlebarn, Aigen and Hörsching, whilst Zeltweg houses the flying school with Pilatus PC-7s. Hörsching has the two remaining SAAB 105 squadrons and Graz is HQ of the Surveillance Wing.

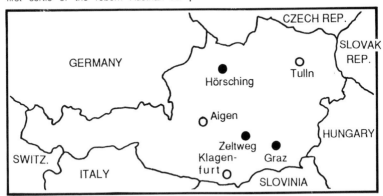

GRAZ/THALERHOF

Location: 6 miles (10km) south of Graz
ICAO code: LOWG
Runways: 17/35 (9,055ft/2,760m);
 17W/35E (grass, 2,100ft/640m);
 17E/35W (grass, 2,493ft/760m)
Also a civil airport, Graz is HQ of the *Überwachungsgeschwader*, or Surveil-lance Wing which, together with an Alouette III wing at Aigen, is a component of *Fliegerregiment II* (2nd Air Regiment) at Zeltweg. The wing is entirely responsible for policing Austrian airspace, for which it has two squadrons of SAAB J-35Oe Drakens: 1 *Staffel*, detached to Zeltweg (where it has an additional training

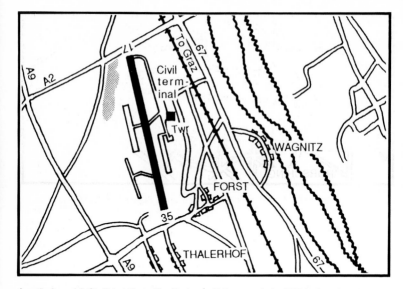

function), and 2 *Staffel* at Graz. The Drakens are upgraded J-35Ds with improved navigation equipment, a J-35F-type clearview canopy and a structural overhaul to ensure a further 1,000 flying hours. Drakens were handed over for training in Sweden during June 1987 and deliveries to Austria began in May 1988.

Drakens operate from a ramp on the west side of the airfield and can be viewed at long range from the public road by the control tower near the civil terminal. A blocked road by the 35 threshold gives good views of landing aircraft. The Osterreichisches Luftfahrtmuseum at Graz is open daily from May to October and includes over 20 aircraft, most of which are civilian lightplanes and gliders.

Military operations at Graz started on 1 May 1957 when the *Jabo-Schulstaffel* (Fighter-bomber Training Squadron) was established with three newly-delivered DH Vampire T55s. Two more were added in 1961, but all transferred to Hörsching in February 1963. In return, the *Fliegerschulkompanie* (Flying School Company) arrived from Hörsching on the 4th of the same month with North American T-6 Texan (Harvard) basic trainers, the last of which was withdrawn in 1968. The unit became II *Schulgeschwader* with two squadrons of Fouga Magisters, of which 2 *Staffel* moved to Zeltweg early in 1968 before the wing disbanded on 1 December 1969. Also resident was a Safir squadron (2/I *Schulgeschwader*) which rejoined the main unit at Zeltweg in 1968.

By way of replacement, Graz became base for the second SAAB J-29 squadron, detached from Linz (which see). Following conversion to red-coded SAAB 105s, the unit adopted its present designation of 2 *Staffel/Überwachungsgeschwader* on 15 October 1976. The wing provided the 'Karo As' four-ship aerobatic team between 1975 and conversion to Drakens.

HÖRSCHING/LINZ

Location: 7½ miles (12km) southeast of Linz
ICAO code: LOWL
Runway: 09/27 (9,219ft/2,810m)

Two air force wings are resident at Hörsching, together forming *Fliegerregiment* III. The *Jagdbombergeschwader* (Fighter-Bomber Wing) has two squadrons of SAAB 105s: 1 *Staffel* (red letter codes) and 3 *Staffel* (green codes) — the individual colouring diluted by blue and red aircraft from II Regiment. Helicopter support is provided by *Hubschraubergeschwader* III with 1 *Staffel* of

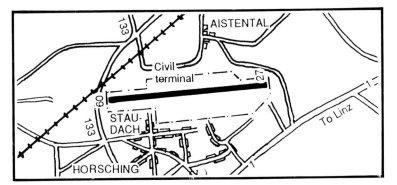

Agusta-Bell 212s and 2 *Staffel* operating ageing AB.204Bs.

Military ramps are on the south side of the airfield. Access to the 27 threshold may be gained by a track from the northern side and views of the military side are also available from here. Access to the 09 end of the runway is best from the blocked road at Staudach. The base has held occasional open days, for example in 1990 and 1993.

Hörsching was first used early in 1957 for a Yak-18 detachment undertaking an advanced pilot training course. However, on 1 October 1957 four Yak-18s from Langenlebarn were permanently transferred, being augmented by five Fiat G.46s in the spring of 1958, these two types became the equipment of Flying School Company 2 (*Fliegerschulkompanie II*), which formed on 1 May 1958. An American gift of 10 North American T-6 Texans in 1960 allowed the Yaks to be withdrawn, followed in 1963 by the G.46s, the Company moving to Graz on 4 February that year.

The association of Hörsching with helicopters was initiated on 28 March 1958 when an initial three Sud Alouette IIs arrived from France for *Hubschrauberstaffel* 1, which formed on 1 April. A month later, on 1 May 1958, Westland WS-55 Whirlwinds were added, followed by Agusta-Bell 204Bs in 1963. However, on 1 October 1964 the squadron split, the AB.204s and WS-55s becoming 3 Helicopter Squadron, although the Whirlwinds were withdrawn late in 1964.

From 1 April 1967 the Bells formed 1 *Staffel* of I *Geschwader* whilst Alouette IIs were 1/II *Geschwader*. Two Sikorsky S-65Oe medium helicopters entered service on 1 September 1970, equipping 2 *Staffel*, but were sold to Israel in May 1981. Meanwhile, 1/I *Staffel* had received Agusta-Bell 212s from 3 May 1980 onwards. The AB.204Bs were put in storage, but eight were soon reissued to 2 *Staffel* as replacements for its S-65s. Alouette IIIs were allocated to 1/II *Staffel* from 28 January 1967, but in a reorganisation of October 1976 they became part of the wing at Aigen and III *Geschwader* formed at Hörsching to administer the local helicopter units.

The base was chosen as the home of Austria's first jet fighters, although the initial 15 SAAB J-29s had to be delivered to Vienna/Schwechat on 6 July 1961 because infrastructure was not complete at Hörsching. The aircraft moved to Linz on 28 May 1962, flown by the 1 Fighter-Bomber Squadron, which had formed on 23 June 1961. Five DH Vampire T55s arrived from Graz in February 1963 and, with 15 more J-29s in prospect, the 1st FB Wing formed on 1 July 1963 and added a second *staffel* at Graz. Following the arrival of three more Vampires, these aircraft were established as 3 *Staffel* from 1966 until the type was withdrawn on 20 April 1972. SAAB 105s were received from 2 July 1970 onwards and the J-29s flew their last sortie on 21 July 1972.

ZELTWEG

Location: ½ mile (1km) N of Zeltweg
ICAO code: LOXZ
Runway: 08/26 (5,249ft/1,600m)

Long associated with training, Zeltweg houses the Pilot School (*Pilotenschule*) operating Pilatus PC-7 Turbo Trainers and

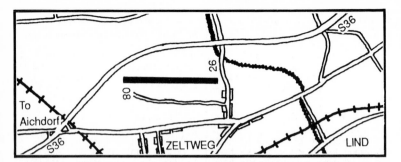

1 *Staffel* of the Surveillance Wing (*Überwachungsgeschwader*) with Drakens.

Geography provides for fine views of aircraft landing over the road at the eastern end of the runway. The Draken dispersal and taxiway are on the north side, close to the 26 threshold. The PC-7s live in a separate area to the south and are slightly less accessible. 1 *Staffel* has a secondary training role, but its operational task gives Zeltweg's mile-long runway the dubious distinction of being one of the shortest in Europe for permanently-based combat aircraft.

An airfield support company formed at Zeltweg in 1956 prior to the arrival in March 1957 of I *Fliegerschulkompanie* with Piper Super Cubs, Zlin 126s and (soon afterwards) Fiat G.46s — the latter going to Hörsching in 1958. The Company became I *Schulgeschwader* shortly before its 1st Squadron received SAAB Safirs on 10 September 1964. A second squadron was based at Graz until it joined the main unit at Zeltweg early in 1968. By this time, a renaming had seen birth of the *Fliegerschule* on 11 October 1976.

Replacement of Safirs by PC-7s began with the arrival of the first six in December 1983 and they were followed by four in November 1984 and the final six in November 1985.

Early in 1968, the Fouga Magisters of 1/II *Schulgeschwader* arrived at Zeltweg as the *Düsenschulstaffel*. The last Magisters were withdrawn on 24 April 1972, but on 4 May that year, the *Düsenschulstaffel* began re-equipping with SAAB 105s wearing blue codes A-J. In an air force reorganisation during 1976, the *Überwachungsgeschwader* was established on 15 October for air defence, the blue-coded SAAB 105s becoming its 1 *Staffel*.

OTHER MILITARY AIR BASES:
- **Aigen-im-Ennstal** 5 miles (8km) SE of Liezen. *HbSchGesch* II (Alouette III).
- **Klagenfurt** 1¾ miles (3km) NE of Klagenfurt. Detachments (Alouette III and OH-58A).
- **Tulln-Langenlebarn** 2½ miles (4 km) E of Tulln. *HbSchGesch* I (AB.212, AB.206, OH-58A, PC-6).

Austrian air bases have much infrastructure remaining from prewar days, as can be seen in the backdrop to this SAAB 105. *via Paul Jackson*

BELGIUM

Following disbandment of the Warsaw Pact, Belgium has reduced by 50% the number of combat aircraft it assigns to NATO: from eight squadrons with 144 F-16 Fighting Falcons and Mirage 5s to six smaller squadrons with 72 F-16s. This could result in the downgrading of Bevekom/Beauvechain in 1994 from a combat base to a training station housing units previously at Brustem and Goetsenhoven/Gossoncourt. Bierset, last home of the Mirage, lost its jets in January 1994 and is receiving army helicopters from Germany (see German section: Butzweilerhof, Merzbrück and Werl).

Only Florennes (2 Wing) and Kleine Brogel (10 Wing) remain as front line, F-16 operating bases, whilst transports are located at Melsbroek, the military side of Brussels/Zaventem airport. Koksijde/Coyxde has SAR and Navy helicopters and is also a storage unit for surplus and withdrawn aircraft, in which role it was joined in October 1993 by the NATO reserve airfield and air cadets' glider base at Weelde, where new hangars have recently been built.

Dual names for some bases and air force units are explained by the fact that Belgium has two principal languages: Flemish (a Dutch dialect), spoken in the north, and French, favoured by the Walloons of the south. Both agree to use the English word 'wing', but the air force is known both as the *Belgische Luchtmacht* and *Force Aérienne Belge* (BLu/FAéB).

Nucleus of the postwar BLu/FAéB were Nos 349 and 350 Squadrons of the RAF, staffed by Belgian personnel. Flying training and technical training schools were formed in the UK and transferred to Belgian soil in 1946. The technical school is now at the non-flying base of Safraanberg (1 mile/2km SE of Brustem by the N3), equipped with some instructional airframes. Of the prewar bases, only Evere was immediately available, whilst Schaffen and Wevelghem were damaged. More promising were *Luftwaffe* airfields at Chievres, Bevekom, Brustem, Florennes

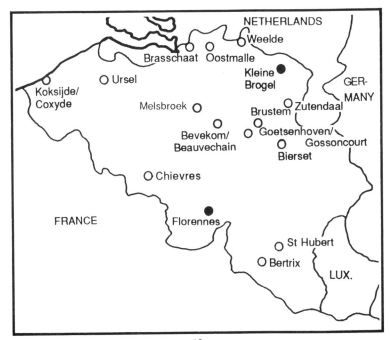

and Melsbroek, all of which became major installations.

Spitfires of Nos 349 and 350 Squadrons left Germany for Bevekom on 24 October 1946 and in June 1949 this became the first jet base when No 350 began equipping with Gloster Meteor F4s. The air force later progressed to Meteor F8s and night-fighter NF11s, but the US became increasingly prominent as the main provider of equipment under NATO auspices and Belgian airfields were well stocked with Republic F-84G Thunderjets and F-84F Thunderstreaks, as well as the RF-84F Thunderflash reconnaissance version.

Strength peaked during the late-1950s when Bevekom, Bierset, Brustem, Chievres, Florennes and Kleine Brogel each had a fighter wing of at least three squadrons. Meteor NF11s were replaced by Avro Canada CF-100 Canucks at Bevekom. In January 1962, Brustem reopened as a training base to house units displaced from Africa after the Congo revolt of 1960.

Bevekom became home to the first wing of Lockheed F-104G Starfighters in 1963 and 100, plus 12 TF-104G trainers, saw service until the last pair made a farewell flypast on 19 September 1983. Mirage 5s entered service in 1970: 63 Mirage 5BAs, 27 5BRs for reconnaissance and 16 5BD trainers flew from Bierset and Florennes until December 1993. Replacing both types, the BLu/FAéB has received 136 F-16As and 24 F-16Bs, the first delivery being to No 349 Squadron at Bevekom on 26 January 1979.

FLORENNES

Location: ½ mile (1km) SE of Florennes
ICAO code: EBFS
Runway: 08/26 (11,114ft/3,388m)

Half of Belgium's fighter strength — 36 Lockheed F-16A/B Fighting Falcons — is based at Florennes, under the control of 2 Wing. Until 1994, these aircraft were flown by two squadrons, of which No 1 has the fin badge of a thistle and No 2 uses a comet. All wear the wing insignia of a black and white quartered diamond on the fin-tip. Following disbandment of

1 Wing at Bevekom, No 350 Squadron is moving to Florennes in 1994, when 12 of the based aircraft will be decorated with a Gallic warrior's head.

Florennes is current home of the NATO Tactical Leadership Programme which provides approximately six courses per year, each lasting three weeks. Around 10 fighter/attack squadrons from several countries participate, each unit bringing at least two aircraft.

Prior permission is required to visit the base's Spitfire Museum, which also

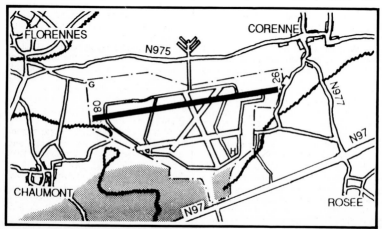

includes five (R)F-84F/Gs and a Mirage 5BR.

There is a 'spotters' corner' lay-by on the road close to the 26 threshold. The road running southwest from Corenne is a good vantage point, but aircraft landing on runway 08 are more difficult to observe. A dispersal north of the N975 is believed to be no longer in use.

Having been built in 1942 under German occupation, Florennes began its postwar career when No 161 Wing formed on 1 November 1946 and worked-up Nos 351 and 352 Squadrons with fighter-bomber Spitfire XIVs. On 1 February 1948, the wing became No 1 to match redesignation of the squadrons as Nos 1 and 2 shortly before. No 3 *Smaldeel/Escadrille* was added in January 1950, also with Spitfires. April 1951 witnessed the arrival of F-84G Thunderjets, which gave way to F-84F Thunderstreaks in August 1955. Florennes was named J. Offenberg air base in August 1956. No 3 Squadron disbanded on 15 October 1960, but Nos 1 and 2 continued flying the increasingly obsolescent F-84s for another decade.

No 8 Squadron formed at Florennes on 15 July 1970 to become the Dassault Mirage 5 OCU — its first task being conversion of No 2 Squadron to Mirage 5BAs in 1971. No 1 moved to Bierset on 2 July 1971, making room for No 42 Squadron and its reconnaissance-tasked Mirage 5BRs, which arrived from Bierset on 15 September 1971. No 8's stay was brief, and it departed for Bierset on 15 December the same year.

Florennes was chosen as the Belgian base for BGM-109G Gryphon cruise missiles of the USAF. The 485th Tactical Missile Wing activated on 1 August 1984 with the 405th TMS (renumbered 71st TMS two weeks later) and received its first four launch vehicles (16 missiles) in March 1985. The build-up was overtaken by the December 1987 INF treaty and all weapons were removed during the following year. Also abandoned were plans for a Belgian civilian consortium to perform routine overhauls at Florennes on all 464 European-based BGM-109s.

No 2 Squadron stood down on 20 December 1987 and began training on F-16s at Kleine Brogel. Its first machine was FA97, delivered on 28 January 1988. After a three-month period at Bevekom, it returned to Florennes in October 1988, following which it was No 42's turn to depart. The squadron left for Bierset, the final Mirage departing Florennes on 25 November 1988. No 1 Squadron returned from Bierset without aircraft in March 1989 (the month that No 2 was declared operational) and began working-up on F-16s, flying its first sortie (with FA117) on 3 July 1989 before being declared operational on 1 July 1990. Pilot training is provided by 'B Flight' which runs six-month fighter-bomber conversion courses.

KLEINE BROGEL

Location: 2½ miles (4km) NNE of Peer
ICAO code: EBBL
Runway: 05/23 (10,158ft/3,096m)

'KB' increased its complement from two to three squadrons of Lockheed F-16A/B Fighting Falcons during 1994 with the addition of No 349 Squadron from the disbanded No 1 Wing. No 349, which has the badge of two crossed 'morning stars' (spiked balls on chains), joined the long-term No 10 Wing components of No 23 Squadron (a devil) and No 31 Squadron (a tiger). The three units share 36 aircraft — the same number as was previously used by the two-squadron wing. In addition, 'B Flight' is responsible for training and has the attractive badge of a pilot's head flanked by a young devil and a tiger cub.

During 1993, 'KB' was reduced to using the parallel taxyway as a runway, as funds did not permit essential repairs on the runway. A short road running southeast from Kleine Brogel village gives access to one dispersal, which can also be glimpsed through trees bordering the N748. A spotters' lay-by has been built on the same road close to the threshold of runway 05. Tracks through the woods off the N747 give access on foot to the 23 threshold. Three Starfighters and four F-84E/Fs are preserved at various locations on the base, together with a Voodoo owned by the Brussels Museum.

Built during the NATO airfield expansion period, 'KB' received its first — and current — resident on 20 March 1953 when No 10 Wing HQ arrived from Chievres. In fact, its component Nos 23, 27 and 31 Squadrons spent much of the next two years at (No 27) Geilenkirchen, (No 23) Brüggen and (No 31) Bierset, Geilenkirchen and Weelde until building

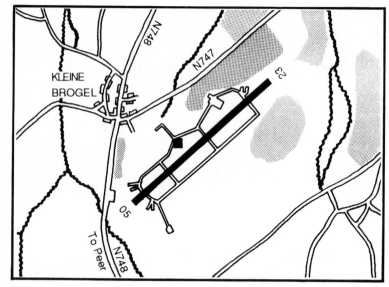

work was complete early in 1955. Equipped at that period with F-84G Thunderjets, No 10 Wing converted to F-84F Thunderstreaks in 1956, No 27 acting as an OCU until disbanded in June 1962. During 1964, Kleine Brogel re-equipped with Lockheed F-104G Starfighters, for which US-supplied tactical nuclear weapons were held on-base by Det 1 of 36th TFW, redesignated 7361st Munitions Maintenance Squadron in 1972.

An OCU Flight formed at 'KB' on 1 December 1981 with six F-16Bs and began training No 23 Squadron, for which the first F-16A (FA39) arrived on 2 December. The squadron was declared operational in March 1983, followed by No 31 in September 1984. Weaponry includes US-owned B61 nuclear bombs.

Twenty years of Belgian Hercules operations were marked by this specially adorned example from Melsbroek. *Paul Jackson*

Rara avis. Just three Alouette IIIs are operated by the Belgian Navy as part of No 40 Sqn at Koksijde/Coxyde.
Paul Jackson

OTHER MILITARY AIR BASES:

- **Bertrix** 3 miles (5km) NW of Bertrix. Reserve airfield and US depot.
- **Bevekom/Beauvechain** S of Beauvechain village. May receive Training & Instruction Group from Gossoncourt (No 5 Sqn, SF.260) and Brustem (9 Wing: Nos 7, 9 & 11 Sqns, Alpha jet; No 33 Sqn, Magister).
- **Bierset** 5½ miles (9km) W of Liege, S of Bierset village. Receiving *Groepering Lichte Vliegwezen/Groupement Avions Légères* from Germany (17 & 18 Battalions, Agusta A.109; 16 Battalion, Alouette II).
- **Brasschaat** 7½ miles (12km) NNE of Antwerp, west of route 117. Army aviation school (Alouette II and A.109).
- **Brustem/St Truiden** immediately SSW of St Truiden. 9 Wing possibly moving to Bevekom; to close.
- **Chievres** 8½ miles (14km) NW of Mons, immediately SE of Chievres village. NATO-assigned; communications airfield for SHAPE at Casteau, near Mons. Detachments (C-9A, UH-1H, UH-60A).
- **Goetsenhoven/Gossoncourt** 1½ miles (3km) SE of Tienen, on eastern side of N64. No 5 Sqn moving to Bevekom in 1994; to close.

- **Koksijde/Coxyde** between Veurne and Koksijde village. No 40 Sqn (SAR Flight, Sea King; Navy Flight, Alouette III). Aircraft storage.
- **Melsbroek** Northern side of Brussels Airport. 15 Wing (No 20 Sqn, Hercules; No 21 Sqn, Falcon 20, BAe 748, Merlin); *Rijkswacht/Gendarmerie* (Alouette II & Puma).
- **Oostmalle** 2½ miles (4km) WSW of Oostmalle. Military gliders. To be sold.
- **St Hubert** (military) 3 miles (5km) NW of St Hubert. Reserve airfield.
- **Ursel** 5 miles (8km) WSW of Maldegem. Reserve airfield.
- **Weelde** 4½ miles (7km) N of Turnhout. Reserve airfield (military gliders; stored Mirages and F-16s).
- **Zutendaal** 3¼ miles (6km) E of Genk. Reserve airfield and US depot.

DENMARK

With disbandment of its second and final SAAB Draken squadron in 1993, Tactical Air Command (*Flyvertaktisk Kommando*) of the *Kongelige Danske Flyvevåbnet* (Royal Danish Air Force) has become an all-F-16 force, operating just four squadrons at two bases: Ålborg and Skrydstrup. Materiel Command (*Flyvemateriel Kommando*) is stationed at Vaerløse, near Copenhagen, with one helicopter SAR squadron and a mixed transport unit with three Lockheed Hercules and three Gulfstream IIIs — the latter aircraft also outfitted for maritime surveillance. There is a flying school (*Flyveskolen*) using SAAB MFI-15s which are also assigned to base flights. Naval Aviation (*Søværnets Flyvetjåneste*) has a flight of Westland Lynx operating from fishery protection frigates and Army Aviation (*Hårens Flyvetjåneste*) flies Hughes 500Ms, SAAB MFI-15 Supporters and a dozen recently-delivered, missile-armed Aerospatiale AS 550C2 Fennecs.

Denmark's role in NATO is to police the Baltic Approaches — an obvious task in view of its geographical position. As a result, it is regularly the host of NATO reinforcement squadrons practising their war role, and maintains a network of auxiliary bases. In total, 12 civil and military airfields have the minimum standard facilities of a 2,950ft (900m) runway, landing lights, operations block and parking.

Having escaped some of the worst devastation of World War 2, Denmark was

able to use a few ex-German facilities when it began rebuilding its air forces. The plural is required, for both army and navy air arms existed until the KDF was formed in October 1950 and the ex-naval *Luftflotiller* were redesignated as *Eskadriller* on 8 January 1951. First postwar equipment comprised six Percival Proctors delivered late in 1945.

Vaerløse and Copenhagen/Kastrup Airport were the bases for some of the early aircraft, although Avnø opened in 1946, flying KZ.II trainers. The first combat base was Karup, where *Esk* 5 of army aviation formed with Spitfire HF.IXs on 1 April 1948. Built by the *Luftwaffe* and previously named Grove, Karup was the true birthplace of the modern KDF, for Nos 723-730 Sqns all formed and worked-up there before most of them moved on to other stations. One of the first was 3 *Luftflotille*, established on 20 October 1949 with Gloster Meteor F4s as Denmark's first jet squadron.

Prewar Ålborg and ex-German Skrydstrup were reopened to accommodate the NATO-funded expansion of the early 1950s and saw the arrival of Meteor NF11s, Hawker Hunters, Republic F-84E/G Thunderjets, RF-84F Thunderflashes, North American F-86 Sabres, NA F-100 Super Sabres and Lockheed F-104G (later CF-104) Starfighters. Most recently, Karup was home to 51 attack/reconnaissance SAAB Drakens, but *Esk* 725 disbanded on 31 December 1991 and *Esk* 729 did likewise on the last day of 1993, apparently ending the airfield's operational career.

Following the 1988 Ramstein air show disaster, Denmark emulated Germany in cutting back air shows. The country now hosts only the occasional event, such as at Ålborg in 1993.

ÅLBORG

Location: 3¼ miles (6km) NW of Ålborg
ICAO code: EKYT
Runways: 08L/26R (8,694ft/2,650m);
   08R/26L (8,694ft/2,650m); 04/22
   (4,593ft/1,400m); 15/33
   (5,906ft/1,800m)

A joint-user airfield, Ålborg has two resident squadrons of F-16A/Bs, differentiation between which is possible only by small badges. *Esk* 723 has a spread falcon (*Jagtfalk*), divided blue and white; *Esk* 726, three falcon-claws conjoined (*Falkatreklo*). The F-16 arrived at the base when No 723 returned from conversion at Skrydstrup on 30 March 1984. Its partner began working-up on the first day of 1986, but did not receive its own aircraft until 1 April 1987. *Esk* 726 took-on a photo-reconnaissance task on 1 January 1994 with retirement of the last Drakens. The base flight has a SAAB MFI-15 on loan from the central pool at Karup.

Flyvestation Ålborg (FSNALB) was designated the RDAF's Gloster Meteor base, its first unit arriving on 16 June 1952 in the form of *Esk* 724 and its Meteor F8s (plus a few Airspeed Oxfords for asymmetric training). The squadron had formed on 8 January 1951 at Karup and it was from here that *Esk* 723 also arrived on 1 December 1952. The same day, the *Flyveskolens Jagerkursus* (Flying School Fighter Course) was established at Ålborg to take over No 723's Meteor F4s and T7s. On arrival, No 723 picked-up five Meteor NF11 radar-equipped night-fighters which had landed at Ålborg on 28 November, and soon built up to an establishment of 20. As the result of heavy losses due to over-rapid expansion, KDF training and administration were revised and the *Jagerkursus* became 'C' Flight of *Esk* 724 on 1 June 1954.

A new day-fighter made an appearance at Ålborg in April 1956 when *Esk* 724 was issued with Hawker Hunter F51s, but the station's fidelity to the UK aircraft industry began to lapse on 10 June 1958 when No 724 went to Karup in exchange for *Esk* 726 and its F-84G Thunderjets. The following month, on 28 July, *Esk* 723 received its first F-86D Sabre all-weather fighter, although it was May 1959 before the last Meteor was withdrawn. Conversion of No 726 to F-86Ds was even more protracted and was accomplished over 13 months from August 1958. Another aircraft which became a regular sight in the Ålborg circuit was the Lockheed T-33A T-Bird. An advanced FTS, the *Traeningsflight*, formed on 6 August 1956 with F-84Gs and quickly added T-33s and DH Chipmunks, both of which were still in use when it moved to Skrydstrup on 15 April 1966.

Denmark's small army aviation force has only recently received its first armed helicopters: Aerospatiale Fennecs with HOT anti-tank missiles. *Paul Jackson*

Danish Hercules have adopted a more purposeful appearance with grey camouflage and ALR-56 radar warning receivers in wingtip pods. *Paul Jackson*

21

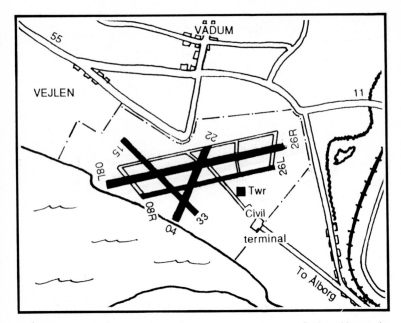

Ålborg was selected to be Denmark's first Mach 2 fighter base when Nos 723 and 726 were earmarked for F-104G Starfighters. *Esk* 726 stood-down for conversion on 30 June 1964 and received its first aircraft by sea in November of that year. No 723 followed in January 1965 and both squadrons later topped-up with former Canadian Starfighters, supplied from 1971 onwards. *Esk* 723 began F-16 conversion on 1 March 1983 and retired its last Starfighter at the end of 1984. The F-104 became extinct at Ålborg when No 726 stood-down on 30 April 1986 to complete its transition to F-16s.

SKRYDSTRUP

Location: 2 miles (3km) SE of Vojens
ICAO code: EKSP
Runway: 11L/29R (9,940ft/3,030m)

The traditions of Skrydstrup as a fighter-bomber base are maintained by the resident F-16A/B squadrons. *Esk* 727 has the badge of Thor's hammer (*Torshammer*) and *Esk* 730, a mythical bull (*Himmeltyren*). Differentiation between squadrons is made slightly easier by the fact that No 727 applies its badge to the fin,

instead of the usual F-16 position on the port side of the engine air intake. An MFI-15 lightplane comprises the base flight.

Skrydstrup has a civil apron and a parallel taxiway 80ft (24m) wide which is available as a secondary runway (11R/29L). Two shelter complexes are in the southeast and southwest corners of the airfield, access to which is possible along several tracks found along the southern boundary road. A hill east of Lillholt gives interesting views of aircraft in the circuit, but it is too far from the base for photography. Nearby, an F-84G may still exist in a playground in Ostergardestr, on the east side of Vojens.

Skrydstrup was known as Haderslev when opened by the *Luftwaffe* in 1944. It passed to Danish control in November 1945 and after rebuilding was the last of the RDAF bases to become operational: it received the final three new squadrons to be formed in the postwar air force. All were formed at Karup with F-84G Thunderjets before arriving at their new home on 1 August 1953 (*Esk* 728), 1 January 1954 (*Esk* 729) and 6 September 1954 (*Esk* 730). Of these, No 728 converted to F-86D Sabre all-weather fighters in July

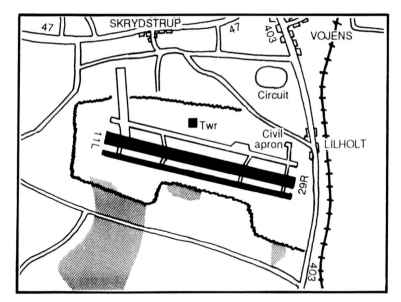

SKRYDSTRUP

VOJENS

Circuit

■Twr

Civil apron

LILHOLT

11L

29R

1960 before disbanding on 31 March 1966, but Nos 727 and 730 brought to Skrydstrup Denmark's first fully supersonic aircraft, the F-100D/F Super Sabre.

After converting at Karup, *Esk* 730 returned to its long-term home on 20 September 1961, whilst No 727 arrived from the same base on 1 April 1974. In the meantime, *Esk* 729 had disbanded on 1 March 1960 and *Esk* 724's Hunters moved-in from Ålborg on 16 March 1959 and remained until they and their unit stood-down on 31 March 1974. A non-operational resident was the *Traening-eskadrille*, whose T-33s and Chipmunks were present between 15 April 1966 and disbandment on the last day of 1974.

An F-16 Flight of *Esk* 727 formed on 1 July 1979 to begin training and FSNSKP became the first Fighting Falcon base when the unit's F-100 element disbanded on 1 April 1981. *Esk* 730 followed suit and withdrew its last F-100 on 11 August 1982.

OTHER MILITARY AIR BASES:
- **Avnø** 9 miles (15km) S of Naestved. *Flyveskolen* (SAAB MFI-15).
- **Karup** 2½ miles (4km) SW of Karup. Non-operational since January 1994. Nominal base of SAAB MFI-15 fleet. Military museum (eight aircraft) open Wednesdays, 13.00-16.30 and first Thursday of the month 15.30-18.00.
- **Tirstrup** 13 miles (21km) SW of Grenå. Reserve airfield/civil.
- **Vaerløse** 11 miles (18km) NW of Copenhagen. *Esk* 721 (Hercules, Gulfstream III, MFI-15); *Esk* 722 (Sikorsky S-61A); naval flight (Lynx).
- **Vandel** 3 miles (5km) SE of Billund. Army aviation (Hughes 500M, Fennec). Reserve airfield.

FRANCE

Moderate cuts in operational strength of the *Armèe de l'Air* (AA) are resulting in the disbandment of some squadrons, but few air bases are to be closed. Instead, the administrative structure is being streamlined by elimination of one stage in the chain of command. The wing (*escadre*), responsible for operations at combat and transport bases, is disappearing between 1993 and 1996, allowing squadrons (*escadrons*) to be controlled directly by their parent Command: Tactical (FATac), Transport (CoTAM), Air Defence (CAFDA), Strategic (CoFAS) and Training (CEAA). Simultaneously, those fighter squadrons not disbanding are increasing strength from 15 aircraft in two flights (*escadrilles*), to 20 in three flights. Consequently, air-

craft are carrying even greater combinations of fin badges than ever before. Fortunately, the code worn by most aircraft readily identifies the operating unit but, in a historical context, it is the *name* of a squadron which carries its traditions: EC 3/2 'Alsace' and EC 3/13 'Alsace' are, therefore, the same unit after transfer from the 3rd squadron of 2 Wing to the third in 13 Wing.

Air bases are given a number and, increasingly, named after a prominent aviator. Numbers begin at 101 for operational stations; 201 for (generally) non-operational; 601 for maintenance units; and 701 for schools. Public identification usually is by double-barrel name, comprising the nearest town followed by the

ARMY & NAVAL AIR BASES

BELGIUM
GERMANY
Lille
Etain LUX
Compiegne
Le Bourget Phalsbourg
Les Mureaux Nancy
Landivisiau
Lanvéoc Rennes
Lann-Bihoue
SWITZERLAND
Bourges
Lyon
ITALY
Valence
Bordeaux Gap
Nimes-Garons
Aix
Dax Frejus
Montauban Luc-Le Cannet
Pau Hyeres
St Mandrier
SPAIN
Aspretto
CORSICA

nearest village. Full names are omitted from maps in this book, but appear below. Stations with combat squadrons also possess a base flight with a few Magisters and, possibly, a Paris.

France was a major air power prior to World War 2 and continues to operate from several bases with a long history. Other installations were built or expanded during the German occupation, and a few in the northeast date from the NATO build-up in the early-1950s. France left the military side of NATO in 1966 and was a slightly late convert to the benefits of hardened shelters. These now exist on most fighter bases, but are neither as substantial nor well-appointed as some in Germany and the UK. Additionally, it will be found that some 'HASs' are merely metal sheds — although their effect upon

the telescope-carrying enthusiast is virtually the same.

A sizeable French element in the RAF and USAAF formed the postwar AA, initially relying heavily on aircraft supplied by those allies. DH Vampires (later built under licence) were the first turbine-engined fighters, delivered to 2 Wing at Dijon in July 1949, and subsequently augmented by a successful series of jets from the Dassault stable: Ouragan, Mystère II, Mystère IV, Super Mystère, Mirage III/5, Mirage F1 and Mirage 2000 — not forgetting the Mirage IV strategic bomber. NATO auspices were responsible for the arrival of F-84G Thunderjets, F/RF-84F Thunderstreaks/flashes, F-86K Sabres and F-100 Super Sabres during the 1950s. Today, the only significant foreign aircraft in the front line are 11 Boeing

C-135FR tankers and four Boeing E-3F Sentries.

Aéronavale — or more fully, the *Aéronautique Navale* of the *Marine Nationale* — concentrates its airfields around the major naval ports of Brest (Atlantic) and Toulon (Mediterranean). Fixed-wing fighters (Dassault Super Étendards and Vought Crusaders) are regularly deployed aboard the two carriers, *Foch* and *Clemenceau*, both of which are home-ported at Toulon. Maritime patrol squadrons are in the process of converting from the Atlantic 1 to Atlantique 2, the short-range units still flying the carrier-capable *Breguet Alizé*. Naval aircraft are flown by autonomous squadrons, designated *Flotille* when in the front line and *Escadrille* for second-line duties.

Removal of forces from southwest Germany has brought about changes in the army's ALAT — *Aviation Légère de l'Armée de Terre*. ALAT has over 600 helicopters, most of which are Aerospatiale Gazelles used for liaison, observation and anti-tank missions. The same manufacturer's Puma is a larger troop-transport, backed by a score of newer Cougar (Super Puma) variants. The aged Alouette II and III will also be seen with second-line units. A combat helicopter regiment (RHC) has up to six *Escadrilles*, each with an average of 10 helicopters.

Most of the major air bases have a public open day every three years or so — either a military *Portes Ouvertes* ('Gates Open') or a *Meeting National de l'Air*. Large bases open in recent years have included, 1991: Mont-de-Marsan, Orléans, Reims and Toul; 1992: Avord, Colmar, Luxeuil and St Dizier; 1993: Cambrai, Cazaux, Cognac, Istres, Toul and Toulouse.

AVORD

Designation: *Base Aérienne* 702 'Captain Georges Madon'
Location: Immediately NW of Avord
ICAO code: LFOA
Runway: 06/24 (11,483ft/3,500m)

Avord retains its training base number despite the presence of an operational element: the four E-3Fs of *Escadron de Détection et de Controle Aeroporté* 36 which constitute France's AEW force. Located in the centre of the country, Avord is a suitable location for aircraft which are tasked with omni-directional surveillance. The AA's Embraer Xingu fleet is based here with *Groupement d'Instruction* 319, the twin-engined conversion unit. Courses are currently 102hr in duration but will be increased to 125hr in 1995. Smaller, and more difficult to find on this large airfield are the Mudry CAP.10 lightplanes and two Fouga Magisters of the *École de Formation Initiale du Personnel Navigant* (EFIPN 307), which gives screening courses to prospective pilots.

The E-3F ramp south of the 24 threshold is visible from the D36 road between the villages of Farges and Avord. The approach to runway 24 is accessible; 06 not so. Parking areas for lighter aircraft are difficult to see. Natives are distinctly hostile.

An aviation camp was established on the Avord military exercise area (which still extends north of the D66) in 1910, but the installations were severely damaged by Allied bombing in 1944 and the base has been rebuilt — most noticeably with a new runway of generous proportions. On 23 May 1945 — a fortnight after VE-Day — formation was authorised at Avord of a twin-conversion unit, the *École de Transformation de Pilotage sur Bimoteurs*, equipped with NC.701 Martinets and Cessna UC-78 Bobcats.

The station became *Base École* 702 in 1947 and began converting to Dassault Flamants in 1951 — adding a C-47 Dakota flight for radio training. On 1 June 1965 the unit was again reorganised as GE 319 and on 22 April 1983 replacement Xingus officially entered service. EFIPN 307 joined the base strength from Aulnat in July 1985, when it gained a pair of Magisters to augment its CAP.10s.

Now severed are the base's links with France's strategic force. EB 1/94 formed

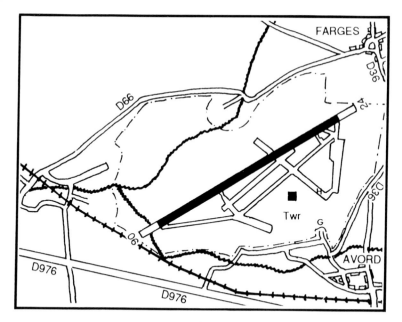

with Mirage IVAs in 1965 and disbanded on 28 November 1986 and ERV 4/94 was established on 1 December 1965 with C-135F tankers. Becoming ERV 2/93 on 1 July 1976 it disappeared on 31 July 1993. EDCA 36 formed on 1 March 1990 and accepted its first E-3F on 22 May 1991.

CAMBRAI-EPINOY

Designation: *Base Aérienne* 103 'René Muchotte'
Location: 5 miles (8km) NW of Cambrai
ICAO code: LFQI
Runway: 10/28 (8,300ft/2,530m)
Long-term resident at Cambrai is the 12th Fighter Wing (12e *Escadre de Chasse*), upgrading of which to Mirage 2000Cs was cut short by defence economies. EC 1/12 'Cambrésis' ('12-Y' codes) returned to the base with its new aircraft on 14 April 1992 after conversion at Dijon and EC 2/12 'Picardie' ('12-Z') was declared operational on the same type on 1 September 1993. EC 3/12 'Cornouaille' remains equipped with Mirage F1Cs and expects to disband in the mid-1990s. EC

1/12 is a NATO Tiger squadron and is the occasional host of 'Tiger Meets'.

Cambrai is a reasonably accessible base, thanks in part to abandoned German facilities. Old runways to the south are outside the fence and give a view of the dump; former dispersals immediately south of Epinoy village are the best place from which to scrutinise the flight-line. The D21E road at the 10 threshold is good for parking and viewing, but poorer parking facilities exist at the 28 end. HAS sites are located in the southeast and southwest corners of the airfield.

A runway was built at Epinoy in October 1939 and the base greatly expanded during the occupation. French DH Mosquitos of GR 1/20 'Lorraine' arrived in June 1946 and remained until the original installations were abandoned in 1951. The following year, reconstruction work — notably on a new runway — began and was sufficiently advanced by 15 March 1953 for a new base commander to be appointed. EC 12 arrived from Mont-de-Marsan on 1 July 1953, bringing its Ouragans.

The wing converted to Mystère IVAs in 1955, Super Mystères in 1959 and Mirage F1Cs from 1976. Strategic associations

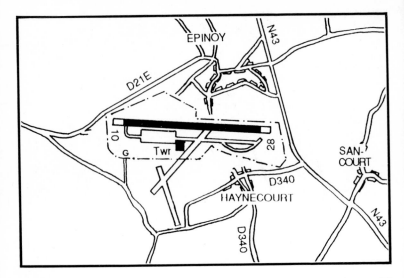

began on 6 July 1965 with formation of EB 3/93 'Sambre', the unit receiving its first Mirage IVA on 1 December the same year. 'Sambre' disbanded in a re-organisation of the strategic forces on 1 July 1976.

CAZAUX

Designation: *Base Aérienne* 120 'Commandant Marzac'
Location: NE shore of Lake Cazaux
ICAO code: LFBC
Runway: 06/24 (7,874ft/2,400m)

Surrounded by weapons ranges, Cazaux is the AA's advanced training base, where students destined for fighter squadrons learn the basics of combat against air and ground targets in 54 flying hours spread over 12 weeks. Principal resident units are two squadrons with Dassault/Dornier Alpha Jet Es: *Escadron de Chasse* 1/8 'Saintonge' (8-M codes) and EC 2/8 'Nice' (8-N). The base flight operates the usual four Magisters but also has a Falcon 20 equipped with target towing. As a result, it has the unique title of ERACLES 09/120 (*Escadron de Remorquage, Accueil, Ciblerie, Entraînement et Support*) (120-F codes). Cazaux houses one of the two squadrons still operating Mirage IVPs: *Escadre de Bombardement* 2/91 'Bre-

tagne'. *Escadron d'Hélicoptères* 1/67 'Pyrénées' has Fennecs and Pumas.

As if the danger areas surrounding the base were not sufficient to deter visitors, Cazaux possesses military police with serious mental problems. Enthusiasts have been arrested, lost film to confiscation, been videotaped for police records and followed by plain-clothes officers — and all that at *public* open days! Very limited views of the Alpha Jet ramp can be obtained from the road north of the camp. Best results are achieved from the beach with a telescope when landings are on Runway 06. Defunct aircraft are used as targets on the ranges, but are strictly out of bounds.

Previously designated *Base École* 706, Cazaux has long been a weapons training station, its previous incumbent being the *Centre de Tir et de Bombardement*. This flew the Anson, Miles Martinet, Wellington and B-26 before gaining jets in the shape of Mistrals, Ouragans and, in 1957, Mystère IVAs (supplemented by a few Meteor NF.11s and other types). On 1 February 1964, the 8e *Escadre de Chasse* formed to replace the CTB, retaining the Mystères until Alpha Jets began arriving in December 1961. HQ EC 8 disbanded on 31 July 1993 and its two squadrons became autonomous. EB 1/92 has been resident since December 1965, flying Mirage IVAs until redeclared operational with ASMP

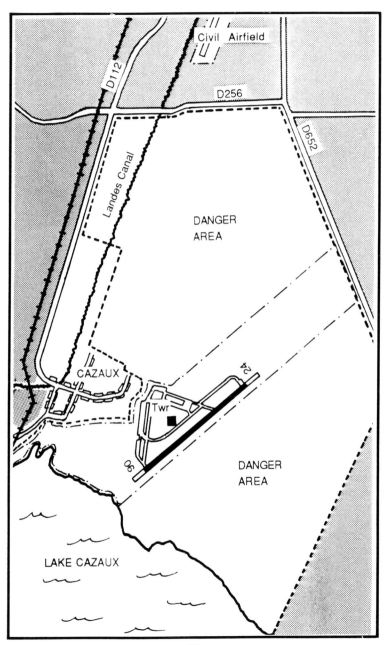

missile-armed IVPs on 1 December 1986. The squadron received Mirage IIIB-RV trainers from the disbanding CIFAS 328 on 1 July 1992, but retired the last three on 2 September 1993. Having functioned under numerous identities, the base/target-towing flight became ERACLES on 1 September 1991.

CHATEAUDUN

Designation: *Base Aérienne* 279 'Lieutenant Beau'
Location: 1 mile (2km) SE of Châteaudun
ICAO code: LFOC
Runway: 10/28 (7,380ft/2,250m)
Despite having only two operational aircraft in residence — the Twin Otters of 70e *Escadron de Convoyage* — Châteaudun is popular with aviation enthusiasts because of its stock of over 200 stored aircraft of 18 types. Main resident is the maintenance unit *Entrepôt de l'Armée de l'Air*. Storage and overhauls are the responsibility of its component, *Moyens Techniques* 10/601, but a fleet of 10 battle damage repair (BDR) airframes (mostly Mirage IIIs) is held by *Équipe d'Études Techniques de Réparation des Dommages dus au Combat* 64/600.

Aircraft stored under cover in serviceable condition are flown every 12 or 24 months, augmenting the activity generated by arrivals and departures. Servicing hangars and the visitors' ramp are on the northwest side of the base, visible from the D955 road. Careful scrutiny from the D955 west of the main gate reveals the BDR aircraft and, if in use, a scrap dump. More machines are parked in the open, south of the active runway, awaiting disposal and many — but not all — are to be seen from the D955 and D31. In 1994, the square Poulmic hangar on the Boirville side was surrounded by 14 Mirage IVAs (mostly obscured by a revetment); 40 Mirage IIIs were on the cross-runway; and 55 Magisters lined the north-south dispersal on the Nivouville side. Several aircraft are preserved around the base. An intermittently-used scrap dump is on the southeast perimeter, by the D31. The site north of the D955 is domestic only — apart from a preserved Super Mystère. Loitering not recommended.

Opened in 1937, Châteaudun has always been an MU, except when in German hands. EAA 601 used the base as an annexe from 1946 until it moved-in from Châteauroux on 1 August 1951, bringing with it the *Escadron de Convoyage*.

COLMAR-MEYENHEIM

Designation: *Base Aérienne* 132 'René Pépin'
Location: 11¾ miles (18km) N of Colmar
ICAO code: LFSC
Runway: 02/20 (7,874ft/2,400m)
France's only wing of Mirage F1CT tactical attack aircraft operates from Colmar with 13e *Escadre de Chasse*. EC 1/13

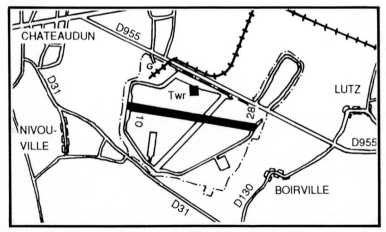

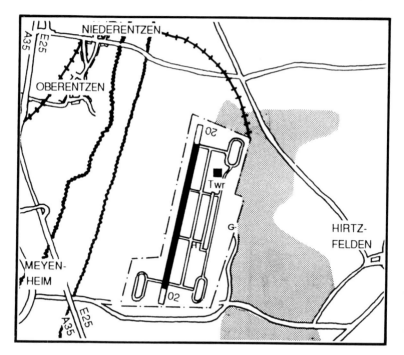

'Normandie-Niemen' (13-Q codes) and EC 3/13 'Alsace' (13-S) have completed conversion, but EC 2/13 'Alpes' retained the Mirage 5F until disbandment in June 1994. The squadrons will be renumbered in 1995, as EC 1/30 'Normandie-Niemen' and EC 2/30 'Alsace'.

The Meyenheim-Hirtzfenlden road affords glimpses of the southeast shelter area, but the southwest HAS site is protected by a mound. Stopping on the road is not advised. Farm tracks from the Niederentzen road give access to the 20 approach.

Construction of Meyenheim began in 1951 and was completed when the air base group moved in on 5 May 1956. However, it was 1 April 1957 before an operational wing arrived in the shape of EC 13 from Lahr, Germany, with two squadrons of F-86K Sabre all-weather interceptors. These were replaced by Mirage IIICs from January 1962 and the AA's first Mirage IIIEs in April 1965, the role now being attack and battlefield air superiority. A third squadron was established with Mirage 5Fs on 1 March 1972

— also the first of this variant to see French service. Later EC 2/13 converted to 5Fs and EC 1/13 also acted as the Mirage III OCU from July 1986.

An instrument flying training unit, *Centre d'Entraînement en Vol Sans Visibilité* 338 was present with T-33As from 1 May 1961 to 1 July 1967. Following training at Mont-de-Marsan, EC 1/13 returned to Colmar with its first Mirage F1CTs on 6 November 1992. EC 3/13 was declared operational with the F1CT in April 1994.

DIJON-LONGVIC

Designation: *Base Aérienne* 102 'Georges Guynemer'
Location: 3¾ miles (6km) SE of Dijon
ICAO code: LFSD
Runways: 02/22 (5,905ft/1,800m); 18/36 (7,874ft/2,400m)

Two squadrons fly Mirage 2000C interceptors from Dijon, providing the air defence of central France. EC 1/2 (2-E codes) is the famous 'Cigognes' (Storks) squadron and is partnered by EC 2/2

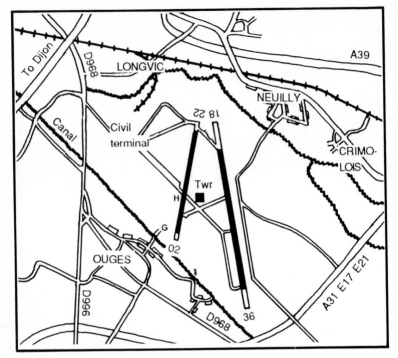

'Côte d'Or' (2-F), the Mirage 2000 OCU. The latter also conducts the first stages of training for Mirage 2000N/D strike/attack pilots, although new interceptor pilots spend two of their three months at Dijon with EC 1/2 gaining weapons experience. EC 2's Mirage 2000Cs are early production machines with RDM radar and M53-5 engines.

Dijon is a joint-user airfield and access can be gained to the civil aviation terminal. Military parking is immediately to the southeast. A lay-by south of the railway and just before Neuilly gives a view of the whole field.

The prewar base at Longvic saw minimal use immediately after the Liberation and initially housed communications unit SLA 41 (Goeland, Ramier and Pinguin). In July 1949 Vampire FB.5s began arriving for the re-formation of EC 2, which moved in from Friedrichshafen, Germany. The wing has been the principal military unit at the base until the present day, its later equipment comprising the Ouragan (from June 1953), Mystère IVA (January 1956),

Mirage IIIC (July 1961 — the first to equip with Mirage IIIs) and Mirage IIIE (September 1968). The first 2000Cs for EC 1/2 flew in on 2 July 1984, making Dijon the initial Mirage 2000 base, and three squadrons had equipped by 1986. However, one of these, EC 3/2 'Alsace' disbanded on 31 July 1993.

EVREUX-FAUVILLE

Designation: *Base Aérienne* 105
Location: 3½ miles (5.5km) E of Evreux
ICAO code: LFOE
Runway: 04/22 (9,810ft/2,990m)

A transport base with a difference, Evreux is also home to several small and unusual units. Main resident is 64e *Escadre de Transport* with two squadrons of Transall C.160NGs: ET 1/64 'Béarn' and ET 2/64 'Anjou'. The secretive 56e *Groupe Aérien Mixte* 'Vaucluse' flies missions for the French security services with Super Pumas and Twin Otters (coded OA-OZ) and a loaned C.160F. In the ELINT role,

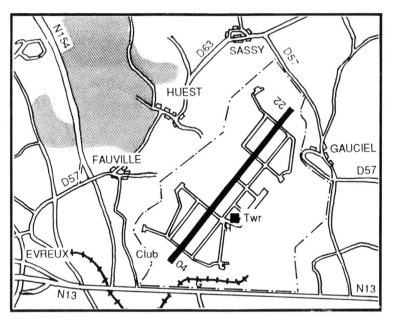

51e *Escadrille Électronique* 'Aubrac' has a single McDonnell Douglas DC-8SARIGUE distinguishable by its wingtip pods. Also non-standard is *Groupe Aérien* 59 'Bigorre' which has four Transall C.160Hs equipped with the Collins TACAMO trailing wire aerial system used for communicating with nuclear missile submarines.

C.160s parked on the southwest side of the airfield can be seen from a track to the aero club which joins Fauville village with the N13. The D63 between Fauville and Sassey gives views of the occasional aircraft. GAM 56's hangar is south of Sassey and the main camp is southwest of Gauciel.

Evreux was assigned to the USAF in October 1952 and began hosting rotational C-119 Packet detachments until the 465th TCW moved in from Toul in May 1955 and stayed until July 1957. Three months earlier, the 317th TCW arrived as a replacement and supplanted its C-119s by C-130 Hercules over the next couple of years. After the 317th left for the USA in June 1964, rotations continued until the 513rd TCW's Hercules were installed during April 1966. With the French withdrawal from NATO then announced, the 513rd moved to Mildenhall in July 1966 and the base reverted to French control in March 1967.

ET 64 transferred to Evreux from Le Bourget on 1 November 1967 with a mixture of Noratlas, DC-6Bs and Breguet 765 Saharas, of which the last-mentioned were withdrawn in 1969, followed by the DC-6s in July 1977. Re-equipment with C.160NGs began in April 1982, allowing the last Noratlas to stand-down in July 1984. GAM 56 was previously based at Persan-Beaumont. EE 51 moved in from Brétigny in 1977 and EE 59 formed on 1 September 1987 before adopting its present title and name on 9 September 1992.

HYERES-LA PALYVESTRE

Location: 1¾ miles (3km) SE of Hyères
ICAO code: LFTH
Runways: 05/23 (6,955ft/2,120m); 14/32 (4,189ft/1,900m)

Combining the delights of aviation and the Riviera beaches, Hyères is the base of naval aviation's deck landing school, 59S (badge: a duck landing on a turtle), with Super Étendards and Zephyrs. Communications for the Mediterranean naval region are the responsibility of 3S (badge: a swan), using Falcon 10s and Nord 262s, whilst the *Escadrille de Réception, de Convoyage et d'Essais* is a ferry and trials unit operating aircraft as required. The *Douanes* (Customs) flies para-military Cessna twins from here.

For training purposes, there are mirror landing aids at the 23 and 32 thresholds. The civil terminal is a good vantage point and it is possible to walk beside the railway line south of the main gate and see through the backs of the hangars. Aircraft landing on Runway 14 can be observed from a blocked road. On the beach it is possible to photograph the 32 approach and other interesting sights.

A long-term naval aviation base, Hyères began the post-liberation period hosting 1F (Spitfire/Seafire) and 3F and 4F (both Dauntless). The two last-mentioned converted to Helldivers in 1950, as did 9F, which arrived in April 1951 and stayed until January 1954. 12F formed from part of 1F on 1 August 1948 and moved-up to Hellcats in 1951. 1F became 11F in August 1953, still with Seafires. 3F disbanded on the last day of 1954, whilst 4F, after flying Avengers at Karouba (Tunisia) returned in 1958 and took on Alizés in 1960. It moved to Lann in July 1964. Amongst other Avenger units, 6F converted to Alizés at Hyères in September 1959, moving to Nîmes in October 1961

and 9F returned to be likewise re-equipped in 1960 before going to Lann in 1970. Meanwhile, 11F received Aquilon jet fighters in April 1955 and moved to Karouba in November 1957 and 12F became a Corsair operator in August 1953 and left for Karouba on 1 January 1956. Similarly, 15F formed in 1953 and took its Corsairs to Telergma in 1956 and 16F was formed with Aquilons on 3 January 1955 — the first with this aircraft.

Two fighter schools were established at Hyères, of which 54S formed on 1 October 1946 and operated Spitfires, Seafires, Dauntless, Helldivers, Hellcats, Aquilons and second-line types for deck-landing training until disbanded in May 1958. The role went to 59S, formed on 1 February 1956 as an all-weather interceptor school equipped with Aquilons and Hellcats. The Étendard era brought the return of 15F, reformed on 1 June 1962 as the first operational squadron, 16F (the sole Étendard IVP squadron) and 17F. The first two moved to Landivisiau in 1967-69 but 17F did not follow until 19 July 1993, having long been converted (5 September 1980) to Super Étendards. 59S gained its present Zephyrs for deck landings as long ago as 1959, but switched from Étendards to Super Étendards in 1991. It also trained Alizé pilots between 1973 and 1989. 3S has been resident since June 1966.

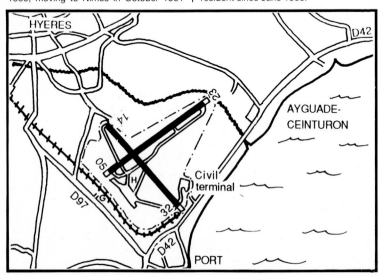

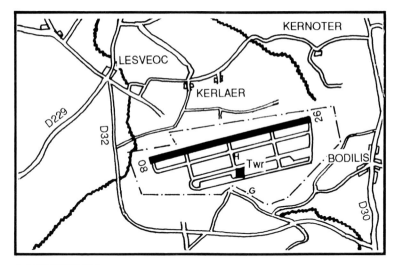

LANDIVISIAU

Location: 3¾ miles (6km) NW of
 Landivisiau
ICAO code: LFRJ
Runway: 08/26 (8,858ft/2,700m)

Landivisiau is the main base for embarked
fixed-wing aviation, despite the fact that
France's two aircraft carriers are home-
ported in the Mediterranean. Super Étendards are flown by 11F (seahorse badge)
and 17F (bird upon an arrow), whilst 12F
operates the remaining F-8E(FN) Crusaders, which are being upgraded for service until the end of the century. They will
be replaced by Rafale Ms, scheduled for a
re-formed 14F. Equally aged are the Étendard IVP photographic reconnaissance
aircraft of 16F (black flamingo). Communications flying and jet proficiency training
is performed by the Paris and Falcon
10MERs of 57S.

Mirror landing aids are at both ends of
the runway; hangars are on the south side
of the airfield. A track from the D32 to
Kerlaer leads to other minor roads on the
north side of the base, whilst the 26
threshold is viewed from a track west of
Bodilis. Good visibility from most areas.

The newest major air base in France,
Landivisiau received its first aircraft on
3 May 1967 when 11F arrived from
Hyères with Étendard IVMs. Similarly-
equipped 15F joined the station in July,
followed by the Étendard IVPs of 16F on
1 April 1968. A second type of naval

fighter was seen on 1 August 1968 when
12F and 14F brought their Crusaders from
Lann-Bihoué. Greatly improved Super
Étendards were first issued to 11F on
4 September 1978, later going to 14F (as
15F had disbanded on 10 January 1969).
However, 14F stood-down on 10 July
1991 and was replaced with the arrival of
17F from Hyères on 19 July 1993. A *Section Fouga* was established on 1 February
1959 with Zephyrs, becoming the Paris-
equipped *Section Réacteur Léger* in May
1972. After adding Falcon 10s in 1975,
the unit adopted its present title of 57S on
1 September 1981.

LANN-BIHOUÉ

Location: 3 miles (5km) W of Lorient
ICAO code: LFRH
Runways: 08/26 (7,874ft/2,400m); 02/20
 (5,479ft/1,670m)

Naval aviation's Atlantic-coast patrol aircraft are stationed at Lann, including the
first Atlantique 2s to enter service. The
fleet is pooled by 23F (badge: a seagull
over a shark) and 24F (a bird over a moor-
ing buoy). Smaller Alizés are flown by 4F.
Of two second-line units, 2S provides
communications for the Atlantic naval
region with Nord 262s, including the
radar-equipped 262E which is also available for SAR. 52S is the naval twin-con-

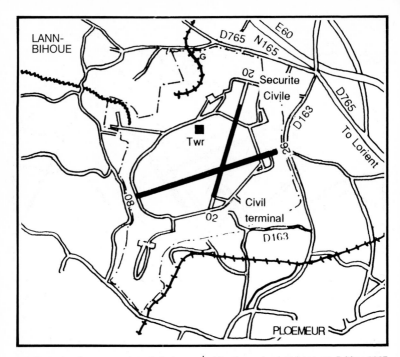

version school, an operator of Embraer EMB-121AN Xingus.

Small, but strategically-placed, woods obstruct the outside observer, but much of the base can be reconnoitred with perseverance. Runway views are good from the civil terminal but yield nothing of the dispersals; hangars can be seen from the east-west section of D163 approaching the terminal. When occupied, the dump is seen from south of the 26 approach. Southwestern dispersals are reached by heading south from the terminal and taking the right turn past the railway to recross the track. Northwest dispersals are reached on foot from a track ¾ mile north of the 08 threshold. Runway 08/26 has mirror landing systems at both ends. A small, private museum includes an Alizé, Neptune and Atlantic.

A wartime base previously rejoicing in the name of Kerlin-Bastard, the present Lann-Bihoué was reactivated in 1951. 25F arrived with Lancasters in October 1953 and converted to Neptunes in June 1958. The same aircraft equipped 23F and 24F when they came from abroad in 1961.

Atlantics arrived at Lann on 5 May 1967 when 24F received its first. 23F re-equipped in 1968 but 25F continued with the Neptune until disbanded on 29 July 1983. In the latest round of modernisation, 23F took delivery of the navy's first three Atlantique 2s on 1 February 1981 and 24F completed its re-equipment on 4 August 1992. Lann acted as the formation base for the two Crusader squadrons (12F on 15 October 1964 and 14F on 1 March 1965) before both were installed at Landivisiau on 1 August 1968. 4F is a longer-term resident, having arrived from Hyères in July 1964 with its present aircraft type. Between 1960 and 1964 radar-training 56S was resident with C-47s, Avengers and Languedocs. *Section Xingu* was established at Lann on the first day of 1983 to usher the new aircraft into service and became 52S on 1 September that year.

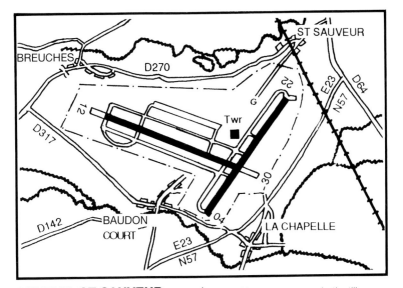

LUXEUIL-ST SAUVEUR

Designation: *Base Aérienne* 116 'Lt Col Papin'
Location: 1¾ miles (3km) SE of Luxeuil
ICAO code: LFSX
Runways: 12/30 (8,343ft/2,543m); 04/22 (7,267ft/2,215m)

Luxeuil is the AA's principal base for manned nuclear strike aircraft and houses two squadrons of Mirage 2000Ns armed with ASMP missiles: EC 1/4 'Dauphiné' (4-A codes) and EC 2/4 'La Fayette' (4-B). Pilots and navigators for the Mirage 2000N, Mirage IVP and (pilot only) Mirage F1CR receive their initial stages of conversion with 339 *Centre d'Instruction Tactique* which has Falcon 20s fitted with appropriate avionics. CITac 339's Jaguars and Alpha Jets provide the first 100 hours of the navigator's course.

Good views of the base and 12 approach and taxiways are possible from tracks running southwards from Breuches, but the D317 is of little use due to mounds and other obstructions. The 30 approach is best viewed from the eastern side of La Chapelle village (including the road which just crosses the stream) as parking on the E23/N57 is difficult. When inhabited, the scrap dump is between the northern ramp and the D270.

Luxeuil is unusual in being a prewar base reconstructed in the early-1950s base with two runways — both still operational. Its first wing was EC 11, which moved in from Lahr in June 1953 with F-84G Thunderjets. These were briefly replaced by F-84F Thunderflashes before the 11 Wing received F-100D Super Sabres in 1958, then moved to Bremgarten, Germany, in the nuclear role during June 1964. This was a straight swap with EC 4, which flew F-84Fs at Luxeuil for two years before gaining Mirage IIIEs in October 1966. Initially armed with AS-30 missiles, the Mirages were issued with French-designed AN52 nuclear bombs late in 1972.

EC 1/4 received its first Mirage 2000Ns on 30 March 1988 and EC 2/4 flew the final Mirage IIIE sortie on 10 November 1988 before converting. The wing transferred from Tactical Command to Strategic Command on 1 September 1991. Departed residents have been the RF-84Fs of ER 1/33 between June 1961 and January 1967 and Mirage IVAs of EB 3/94 'Arbois' from 1 February 1966 until 1983. CITac 339 was formed on 1 July 1988 by redesignation of 339e *Centre du Prédiction et d'Instruction Radar*, a Luxeuil resident since its first Falcon 20 was delivered on 1 March 1969.

Standard French military hangars are easily recognised, but those at Brétigny-sur-Orge, the CEV trials base, have the additional feature of being named after personalities from the test-flying world. Dayglow-finned Mirage IIIR No 306 is part of the trials fleet. *Jean-Louis Gaynecoetche*

Training bases are not as enthusiastic at concealing their aircraft as are their operational counterparts, although these Alpha Jets of the *École de Chasse* at Tours are specially parked for a publicity photograph. Note the unusually large control tower. *Dassault*

Landivisiau is the home base for the French Navy's embarked fighters, including Super Étendards of 17F. A mirror landing aid is installed at both ends of the runway for training.
Paul Jackson

The usual French HAS — here at St Dizier — has a single, sliding door and little accommodation for ground equipment. Completing the picture are two Jaguar As of EC 7.
Paul Jackson

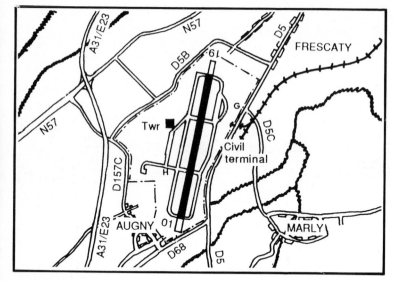

METZ-FRESCATY

Designation: *Base Aérienne* 128
Location: 3¾ miles (6km) SW of Metz
ICAO code: LFSF
Runway: 01/19 (7,874ft/2,400m)

No longer a busy fighter base, Metz has a pair of rare residents in the shape of the C.160G GABRIELs of 54e *Escadre Électronique Tactique*. These Transalls are readily distinguished by their wingtip pods, retractable under-fuselage radome and assorted bumps and aerials for electronic intelligence-gathering. Communications for the 1ere *Commandement Aérienne Tactique* HQ at Metz are the responsibility of another resident, 41e *Escadron de Transport et d'Entraînement* 'Verdun', flying Nord 262s and Paris. Its helicopter equivalent is EH 2/67 'Valmy', with five AS.555 Fennecs and three Alouette IIIs.

Views of aircraft movements are to be obtained from the civil terminal, north of which is the EET 54 ramp. The helicopters reside in the dispersal north of Augny, but are impossible to see from the D157C because of mounds and other obstructions.

F-84G Thunderjets of EC 9 flew into Metz from Lahr in May 1956 and two months later began giving way to F-84F Thunderstreaks. These remained at Metz until the wing disbanded on 1 July 1965

— the penultimate AA unit to fly F-84s. The specially-equipped N.2501 GABRIEL Noratlases of EE 54 also hailed from Lahr when they moved to Metz in July 1966. The type flew its last mission on 26 October 1989, having been replaced by the C.160Gs delivered to the AA from 3 January 1989. The aircraft are flown by *Escadron Électronique* 1/54 'Dunkerque'. EH 2/67 has resided at Metz since September 1972, when it moved from St Dizier, equipped with Alouette IIs and H-34s. The latter were replaced by Alouette IIIs from 21 November 1973, the Alouette IIs more recently giving way to Fennecs.

MONT-DE-MARSAN

Designation: *Base Aérienne* 118 'Col K.W. Rozanoff'
Location: Immediately N of Mont-de-Marsan
ICAO code: LFBM
Runway: 09/27 (11,811ft/3,600m)

Despite being a northern suburb of Mont-de-Marsan, BA118 is a most secret base housing the AA's main experimental unit, *Centre d'Expériences Aériennes Militaires* 330. The two flying components of CEAM 330 are *Escadron de Chasse* 5/330 'Côte d'Argent' (Mirage F1, Mirage 2000) and

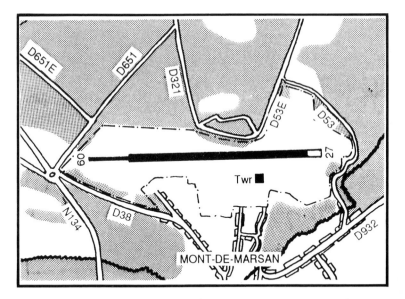

Escadrille d'Expérimentation et de Transport 6/330 'Albret' (transports and support). The first squadron to operate a new
type of aircraft usually works-up at CEAM
before returning to its base. Mont-de-
Marsan is also a base of the Strategic
Forces, with Escadron de Bombardement
1/91 'Gascogne' and its ASMP-armed
Mirage IVPs. Escadrille Électronique 21/54
(part of EE 1/54 at Metz) moved its single
ELINT Puma from Goslar, Germany, in
May 1992.

Large numbers of trees within the base
(not all shown on the map) make observation of activities most difficult, as does an
enthusiastic police force. Fortunately, the
BA118 does hold occasional open days.

Formed in 1947, CEAM has under-
taken trials of virtually every type of aircraft used
by the AA since then and been the host of
detachments from most operational
wings. France's first jet conversion unit,
the Centre de Transformation sur Avion a
Réaction, was established at BA118 on
18 December 1948 with the initial five
French Vampire F1s, delivered from the
UK two days earlier. Recent tasks have
included working-up EC 1/3 with Mirage
2000Ds and ET 1/62 with CN.235s. EB
1/91 was the first Mirage IVA squadron
when formed on 1 June 1964 and con-
ducted the initial drop of a French atomic

bomb in the Pacific on 9 July 1966. The
aircraft used, No 9, is now preserved in
the museum at Le Bourget. After converting to Mirage IVPs, EB 1/91 was declared
operational with ASMP on 1 May 1986. Its
supporting C-135 tankers were operated
by 'Landes' squadron, formed on 1 January 1964 as ERV 1/90 and later designated ERV 4/91 on 1 June 1965 and ERV
3/93 on 1 July 1976. 'Landes' left BA118
for Istres on 5 September 1991.

NANCY-OCHEY
Designation: Base Aérienne 133 'Henri
Jeandel'
Location: 13¾ miles (22km) SW of Nancy
ICAO code: LFSO
Runway: 02/20 (7,992ft/2,436m)
By 1996, Nancy will have completed re-
equipment of its three squadrons to the
Mirage 2000D and will be the sole base
operating the conventional attack version
of this aircraft. EC 1/3 'Navarre' (3-I
codes) returned to the base early in 1994
after conversion, joining EC 2/3 'Champagne' (3-J) which has interim equipment
of Mirage 2000N-K2s and will receive
2000Ds in 1995-96. EC 3/3 'Ardennes'
(3-X) was the last French Mirage IIIE

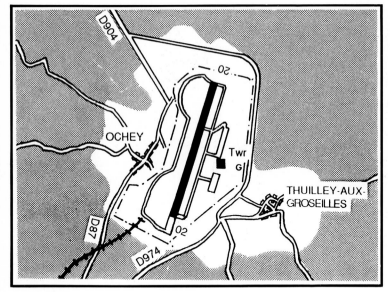

squadron when it stood-down for 2000D conversion in June 1994.

Limited views are available on the northern approach, but the east side of the base is on higher ground than the D974. ECs 1/3 and 2/3 fly from the northeast ramp; EC 3/3 from the southwest HAS site. The field can be seen from the road immediately north of the village of Ochey.

The new base at Ochey received its first residents on 1 December 1961 when the 7e *Brigade Aérienne* arrived from North Africa with three squadrons of Mystère IVAs. Designated EC 7 from March 1962, the wing detached one squadron to Cazaux as the basis of EC 8 in February 1964. In preparation for conversion to Jaguars, the wing transferred to St Dizier on 17 May 1973 and was immediately replaced at BA133 by the T-33As of blind flying training unit, CEVSV 338, which eventually disbanded on 1 July 1982. Unusually, Ochey was the home of two wings for over five years, having gained EC 3 from Lahr, Germany, in September 1967. Equipped with two squadrons of Mirage IIIEs, the wing formed EC 3/3 with Mirage 5Fs on 1 July 1974, re-equipping its newest component with Jaguars in April 1977, then Mirage IIIEs in July 1987. EC 2/3 commissioned with Mirage

2000Ns on 30 August 1991 and EC 1/3 gained IOC with its first six 2000Ds at Mont-de-Marsan on 29 July 1993.

NIMES-GARONS
Location: 6 miles (10km) SE of Nîmes
ICAO code: LFTW
Runway: 18/36 (8,005ft/2,440m)
Maritime patrol over the Mediterranean is undertaken from the *Aéronavale* base at Nîmes, which is home of two squadrons of Atlantics and one of Alizés. 21F and 22F have previously pooled their Atlantic 1s, but 21F (badge: a gazelle's head) begins Atlantique 2 conversion in 1994. Transformation of 22F (three birds over a sunset) was due in 1998, but defence cuts make this unlikely unless all Atlantique 2 squadrons are reduced in size. Veteran Alizés are flown by 6F (Cross of Lorraine) which took over the pilot training task from 59S at Hyères in September 1989. Navigator, air engineer and AEO training is undertaken for the *Aéronavale* by 56S and its belly radar-equipped Nord 262Es.

The civil terminal and car park are well positioned for observation of the naval ramps on the west side of the runway. An Alizé and Dakota are preserved by the navy gate.

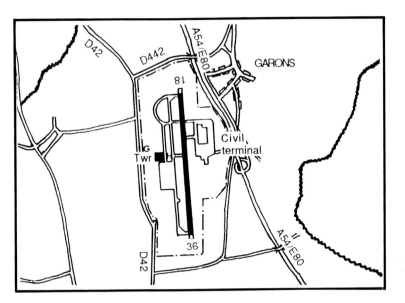

Nîmes appears to be popular with its resident units, none of which has left since arrival. 6F flew-in from Hyères on 1 October 1961, followed by 21F and 22F from Lartigue, Algeria, with their Neptunes. France's first Atlantic 1s were delivered to 21F in December 1965 and to 22F in the following year. The station's training role began when 56S was posted from Lann-Bihoué on 1 April 1964 with Beech JRB-4s and Dakotas. Its initial radar-equipped Nord 262E was accepted on 13 December 1982 and the last Dakotas in French military service were withdrawn two years later.

ORANGE-CARITAT

Designation: *Base Aérienne* 115 'Capt Maurice de Seynes'
Location: 2½ miles (4km) E of Orange
ICAO code: LFMO
Runway: 15/33 (7,896ft/2,407m)

Air defence of southern France is the responsibility of BA115 and its long-term resident, 5e *Escadre de Chasse*. The wing currently has three squadrons: EC 1/5 'Vendée' (5-N codes); EC 2/5 'Ile de France' (5-O); and EC 3/5 'Comtat Venaissin' (5-A), each with 15 Mirage 2000Cs (and a few 2000Bs). Like Cam-

brai, Orange has the later type of Mirage 2000C with RDI radar and M53-P2 engines. It is probable that wing HQ will be disbanded in the near future and strength reorganised as two squadrons of 20 aircraft. The base is also a wartime detachment of EB 1/91 at Mont-de-Marsan.

Orange's two approaches are open for photography from roads at the north of 15 and south of 33, but earth mounds obscure the hangars and flight-line around the southwest ramp.

Returning from Indo-China, EC 5 settled at Orange in August 1950 to re-equip with Vampire FB.5s. The French-built Mistral version followed in April 1954, after which the wing progressed through the Mystère IIC (August 1956), Mystère IVA (January 1958), Super Mystère (April 1961), Mirage IIIC (July 1966) and Mirage F1C (March 1975). EC 3/5 formed as an OCU with two-seat F1Bs on 1 April 1981, but became a regular interceptor squadron with F1Cs in July 1988 and flew the wing's last F1 sortie on 25 July 1990. Meanwhile, EC 1/5 re-formed with 2000Cs on 1 September 1988, to be followed by the other two squadrons. BA115's role as a detachment of EB 1/91 originated in formation of EB 2/93 'Cévennes' with nuclear-strike Mirage

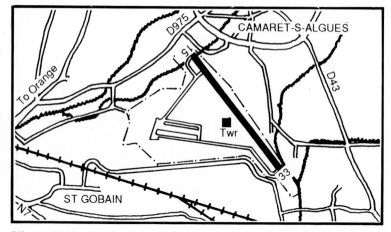

IVAs on 29 March 1965. The squadron became EB 3/91 on 1 July 1976 and disbanded on 1 October 1983.

ORLÉANS-BRICY

Designation: *Base Aérienne* 123
Location: 8¾ miles (14km) NW of Orléans
ICAO code: LFOJ
Runways: 07/25 (7,874ft/2,400m); 04/22 (3,281ft/1,000m) grass

France's first-generation Transall C.160Fs are based at Orléans (with the exception of a handful detached to other units) as are all the more recently-received Hercules. *Escadrons de Transporte* 1/61 'Touraine' and 3/61 'Poitou' share the C.160 pool, whilst the nine C-130H-30s and three standard-length C-130Hs are with ET 2/61 'Franche Comte'.

A track south of the 07 threshold is useful for a brief inspection, but loitering is not recommended; a less hurried view is available from the side-road south of Clos-Aubry if a good telescope is available. There is a lay-by under the 25 approach south of Bricy village from where the ramps are visible; a long stay here can attract attention.

Bricy began its postwar career with a single squadron of Dakotas (GT I/15 'Touraine' attached to ET 61 when it formed at Chartres on 1 April 1946. The squadron became GT 1/61 on 1 July 1947, whilst in October 1953, HQ ET 61 moved into Bricy and the wing began replacing its Dakotas and Ju52 Toucans

with French-designed Noratlases two months later. The first Transall C.160 arrived for ET 1/61 on 22 November 1967, its companion squadrons being similarly outfitted during 1969-70. Delivery of new-generation Transalls to ET 64 was insufficient to fill France's strategic transport gap and so EC 2/61 accepted its first C-130H in the USA on 7 December 1987. The stretched version was added from 5 October 1988 and EC 2/61 now operates only the C-130.

REIMS-CHAMPAGNE

Designation: *Base Aérienne* 112 'Marin la Meslée'
Location: 3 miles (5km) N of Reims
ICAO code: LFSR
Runway: 07/25 (8,136ft/2,480m)

Home of the 30e *Escadre de Chasse*, Reims has two squadrons of Mirage F1s and detaches a third (EC 4/30 'Vexin') to Djibouti. Currently resident are EC 3/33 'Lorraine' (33-F), the F1B-equipped OCU and the two Mirage F1CR reconnaissance squadrons from Strasbourg: ER 1/33 'Belfort' (33-C) and ER 2/33 'Savoie' (33-N) which arrived on 24 May and 22 April 1994, respectively.

Best vantage point is the civil terminal. A track from here runs down the southeast fence, past the tower towards the HAS area. On the west side, the old RD366 road beside the ramps is closed to the public and all traffic is directed on to

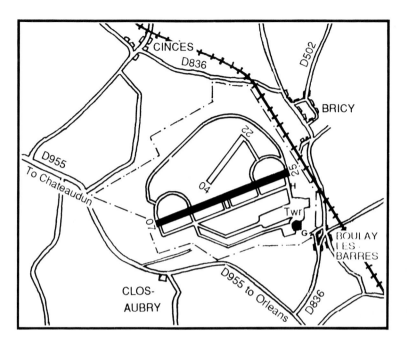

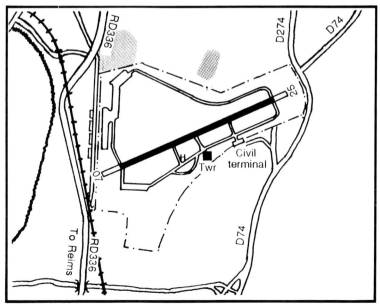

the new road on the opposite side of the railway.

BA112 stands on the site of Reims-Betheny aerodrome which hosted the historic Week of Aviation in August 1909. Used by RAF squadrons in 1939-40 and by the Germans thereafter, it was heavily damaged in 1944 and then used as an American storage depot until 1950. The base's current suffix reflects its role as the airport of the Champagne region. EC 3 arrived from Indo-China in September 1950 and began equipping with Vampires, only to lose them in favour of F-84G Thunderjets in May 1951. F-84F Thunderstreaks next graced BA112's ramps until F-100Ds took over in January 1959. The wing left for Lahr, Germany, in June 1961, three months after Reims began the move to all-weather air defence with the arrival of EC 30 and its Vautour IINs. (Meteor NF.11s of CITT 346 were used for training until October 1963.)

Mirage F1Cs were received by EC 30 from 20 December 1973 onwards. 'Valois' joined the wing from Creil in June 1985 and 'Vexin' formed on 1 July 1988, but EC 2/30 'Normandie-Niemen' disbanded on 31 July 1993. During this period, Reims was also a transport base, beginning in December 1961 with the arrival of ET 2/62 and its Noratlases. The similarly-equipped ET 1/62 joined it on 1 October 1964. Between 1 August 1970 and August 1974, ET 3/62 'Ventoux' operated four Breguet 941S STOL transports from Reims on service trials, but no further purchases

ensued. ET 62 and its two squadrons disbanded on 1 July 1978, and EC 30 followed on 1 July 1994.

ST DIZIER-ROBINSON

Designation: *Base Aérienne* 113 'Cdt Antoine de Saint-Exupéry'
Location: Immediately SW of St Dizier
ICAO code: LFSI
Runway: 12/30 (7,872ft/2,400m)

Reports of a forthcoming run-down of the Jaguar fleet cast a shadow over St Dizier, where half the AA's force is located with EC 7. Components of the wing are EC 1/7 'Provence' (7-H codes); EC 2/7 'Argonne' (7-P), the Jaguar OCU; and EC 3/7 'Languedoc' (7-I). The wing is tasked with conventional attack following withdrawal of its AN52 nuclear weapons on 1 September 1991.

Views of the airfield are obtained from the north side, including the road to the aero club (near which is the road 'Chemin du Robinson', running south of the canal). A turn off the N14/E17 near a garage emerges north-centre of the field — but beware the old woman in a nearby house who calls the police at the first flourish of a telescope! A track originating near Halignicourt exists by the 12 approach, again on its north side.

St Dizier opened on 1 February 1953 when EC 1 arrived from Lahr, Germany, with F-84G Thunderjets. Converting to F-84F Thunderstreaks from August 1955, the wing continued flying from BA113

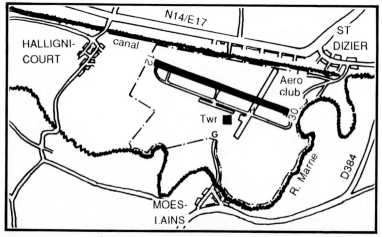

46

until France's last F-84s disappeared with disbandment of EC 1 on 28 February 1966. In later years, F-84s had co-existed with the Alouette IIs and Sikorsky H-34s of EH 23, which arrived from North Africa on 29 July 1962. The helicopters at St Dizier became EH 2/67 on 31 August 1964, but moved out to Metz on 1 September 1972.

On 1 October 1965, EB 2/94 'Marne' was established with Mirage IVAs in a compound at the southeastern end of the field, St Dizier's strategic associations lasting until 1 December 1986, when the squadron disbanded. CEVSV 338 and its T-33As was present between 1 July 1967 and 16 May 1973. The following day, EC 7 (Mystère IVA) moved in from Nancy on 17 May 1973 and took delivery of its first Jaguars seven days later for re-equipment of EC 1/7. EC 3/7 was converted early in 1974 and EC 2/7 formed as an OCU on 11 October that year.

TOUL-ROSIERES

Designation: *Base Aérienne* 136 'Col Georges Phelut'
Location: 8¾ miles (14km) NW of Toul

ICAO code: LFSL
Runway: 04/22 (7,874ft/2,400m)

Three Jaguar squadrons are based at Toul in the conventional attack role, with duties including overseas reinforcement. A reduction in strength is likely in the mid-1990s, but for the moment, the residents comprise EC 1/11 'Roussillon' (11-E codes); EC 2/11 'Vosges' (11-M); and EC 3/11 'Corse' (11-R).

The base is reasonably open from the N41, except that no parking is permitted on this road. A track from Rosieres village leads to the 22 threshold and provides a view into revetments on the east side of the runway at about the centre point. Another track from the N41 skirts the southern boundary and passes under the 04 threshold. No known access from the west, where are located the main camp and HAS sites.

American rights to the use of newly-built Toul were obtained late in 1951 and the 117th TRW (ANG) moved in on 1 February 1952 with RF-80 Shooting Stars. On 10 July 1952 the wing was redesignated 10th TRW, but transferred to Spangdahlem in May 1953. From December 1953 to May 1955, Toul was a trans-

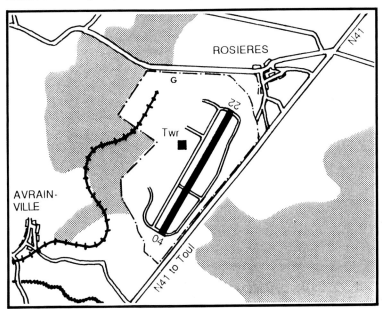

port station hosting C-119 Packets of the 465th TCW, which left for Evreux.

The base returned to fighter operations when the 50th TFW's F-86 Sabres came from Hahn in July 1956, these giving way to F-100 Super Sabres before the wing returned whence it came in December 1959. F-84Fs of the 110th TFS/ANG arrived in November 1961 for the Berlin Crisis, coming under the provisional 7131st TFW until withdrawn in mid-1962. From July 1962 the 10th TRW (then in the UK) detached two of its four RB-66C squadrons (19th and 42nd) to Toul. Introduction to Toul of the RF-4C Phantom was a complex business, involving several squadron changes (bringing a passing acquaintance with the RF-101 Voodoo) and formation of the 26th TRW at Toul as parent unit on 1 July 1965. The wing grew to encompass the 22nd, 32nd and 38th TRSs until, following France's withdrawal from NATO, the 26th transferred to Ramstein in October 1966.

Toul reverted to French control in March 1967 and EC 11 moved-in from Bremgarten on 13 September that year with three squadrons of F-100D Super Sabres. Conversion to Jaguars began with arrival of the first aircraft on 7 February 1975 and on 23 June 1977 the last F-100D left the base for preservation at the *Musée de l'Air*. Jaguars have been despatched on several occasions to back French military operations in Africa and, more recently, participated in the 1991 Gulf War.

OTHER MILITARY AIR BASES:

● **Aix-les Milles** (BA114) 4¼ miles (7km) SE of Aix. ETE 44 (N262, Xingu); EH 5/67 (Puma, Alouette III, Fennec); Commandement ALAT Sud (Alouette II).

● **Amberieu-en-Bugay** (BA273) 1¾ miles (3km) NW of Amberieu. (Sailplanes)

● **Apt-St Christol** (BA200) 14¼ miles (23km) NNE of Apt. EH 4/67 (Puma, Fennec); (Sailplanes).

● **Aspretto** 3 miles (5km) E of Aspretto. 55S (Nord 262).

● **Aulnat** 3¾ miles (6km) E of Clermont-Ferrand. AIA (aircraft overhaul).

● **Bordeaux-Mérignac** (BA106) Immediately W of Bordeaux. ETE 43 (N262, TBM700). Dassault factory.

● **Bordeaux-Souge** 11 miles (18km) W of Bordeaux, 1 mile (2km) NW of Martignas. 4 GHL (Alouette II).

● **Bourges** Immediately SW of Bourges. ALAT central depot (all types).

● **Le Bourget-Dugny** 8¾ miles (14km) NE of Paris. 11S (Xingu, Nord 262). Musée de l'Air.

● **Brétigny-sur-Orge** 17½ miles (28km) SSW of Paris. *Centre d'Essais en Vol* (various types).

● **Cognac-Châteaubernard** 1¾ miles (3km) S of Cognac. (BE709) GE 315 (Epsilon).

● **Compiègne** 1 mile (2km) NW of Compiègne. 6 RHCCA (Gazelle, Puma).

● **Creil** (BA110) Immediately E of Creil. ET 1/62 (CN.235 and Fennec; plus Twin Otter from Sept 1994).

● **Dax** Immediately SW of Dax. *École de Spécialisation* ALAT (Alouette II, Gazelle).

● **Etain-Rouvres** 1 mile (2km) NE of Etain. 3 RHC (Gazelle, Puma).

● **Frejus-St Raphael** 1 mile (2km) SE of Frejus. 20S (Alouette II/III, Super Frelon, Lynx).

● **Gap-Tallard** 1¾ miles (3km) NE of Tallard. 3 Esc/5 GHL (Alouette III).

● **Grenoble-le Versoud** 6¼ miles (10km) NE of Grenoble. EPA 349 (Abeille, sailplanes).

● **Istres-Le Tube** (BA125) Immediately W of Istres. ERV 1/93 & EIRV 3/93 (C-135FR); *Centre d'Essais en Vol* (various); *École du Personnel Navigant d'Essais et de Réception* (various — test pilots' school).

● **Lanvéoc-Poulmic** West of Lanvéoc. 32F (Super Frelon); 34F (Lynx), 35F (Alouette III, Panther), 22S (Alouette II/III); 50S (Rallye).

● **Luc-Le Cannet des Maures** 3 miles (5km) ESE of Le Luc. *École d'Application* ALAT (Alouette II, Gazelle, Puma, Cougar, Fennec).

● **Lille-Lesquin** 5 miles (8km) SE of Lille. 1 Esc/6 RHCCA (Alouette III).

● **Lyon-Corbas** 8 miles (13km) SE of Lyon. 1 Esc/5 GHL (Alouette II).

● **Montauban** Immediately NW of Montauban (82). Det 4 GHL (Alouette II).

● **Les Mureaux** 1 mile (2km) E of Les Mureaux. 1 GHL (Gazelle, Alouette II/III).

● **Nancy-Essey** Immediately W of Nancy. 1 Esc/4 RHM (Gazelle).

● **Pau-Uzein** 5½ miles (9km) NNW of Pau. 4 Esc/4 RHCM (Puma); 5 RHC (Gazelle, Puma).

● **Phalsbourg-Bourscheid** 2½ miles (4km) W of Phalsbourg. 1 RHC (Gazelle,

Puma), 2,3,5 Esc/4RHCM (Puma, Cougar); 2 RHCCA (Gazelle, Puma).

- **Rennes-St Jacques** 3¾ miles (6km) SW of Rennes. 3 GHL (Alouette III, Caravan II).

- **Rochefort-St Agnant** (BE721) 3 miles (5km) S of Rochefort. (Sailplanes and instructional airframes — AA)

- **Rochefort-Soubise** Immediately SE of Rochefort. 51S (CAP10); (Instructional airframes — navy).

- **Romorantin-Lanthenay** 3¾ miles (6km) SE of Romorantin. CVV 55/273 (Abeille and sailplanes).

- **Saintes-Thénac** (BE722) 3 miles (5km) S of Saintes. (Abeille and sailplanes; instructional airframes)

- **St Mandrier** S shore of Toulon harbour. 31F (Lynx); 33F (Super Frelon), 23S (Alouette III, Dauphin).

- **Salon-de-Provence** (BE701) Immediately SSW of Salon-de-Provence. GI 312 (Alpha Jet, CAP 10/230, Magister, Mousquetaire, sailplanes)

- **Solenzara** 4¼ miles (7km) N of Solenzara. EH 6/67 (Puma, Fennec); (sailplanes).

- **Strasbourg-Entzheim/International** (BA124) 6 miles (10km) SE of Strasbourg. Military base closed.

- **Toulouse-Francazal** (BA101) 5 miles (8km) SW of Toulouse. CIET 340 (C.160F); CIEH 341 (Alouette II/III, Puma, Fennec); ENOSA 316 (Nord 262, Paris, Alpha Jet).

- **Tours-St Symphorien** (BE705) 3 miles (5km) NE of Tours. GE314 (Alpha Jet).

- **Valence-Chabeuil** 3¾ miles (6km) E of Valence (26). GALSTA (several — ALAT trials unit).

- **Villacoublay-Vélizy** (BA107) 8¾ miles (14km) SE of Paris. GLAM 1/60 (Falcon 50/900, Super Puma); ET 3/60 (DC-8 at Roissy IAP); ETEC 65 (Falcon 20, Nord 262, Twin Otter, TBM700); EH 3/67 (Alouette III, Ecureuil, Fennec); Commandement ALAT (Alouette II).

GERMANY

Nowhere has the ending of the Cold War had a more profound effect than upon the military bases of Germany. Unification of the two Germanies on 3 October 1990 was the first step in a massive reduction and realignment of forces which has had ramifications throughout the Northern Hemisphere. By the end of 1994, when the last Russian units depart, the former East Germany will be a military wilderness, denuded also of all bar two dozen of the combat aircraft previously flown by the indigenous *Luftstreitkräfte und Luftverteidigung*.

On both sides of the former Iron Curtain, heavily-protected air bases are falling into disuse. Reduced numbers of USAF and RAF aircraft continue to fly in the west, although it can only be a matter of time before the German government requests their departure. The *Luftwaffe* is taking over just two eastern bases, where visitors will be able to compare the style of military architecture with that in the

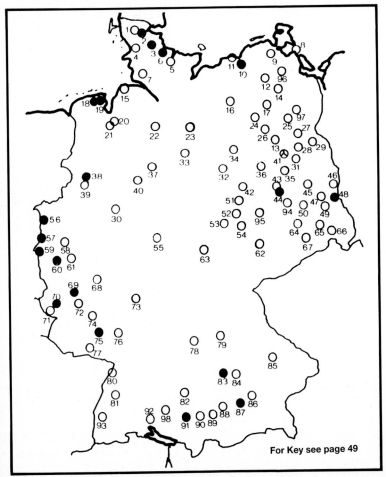

For Key see page 49

remainder of Germany.

Air shows in Germany have been drastically curtailed since the disaster at Ramstein in 1988. The most absorbing since then have been the impromptu events staged by some Russian units before their departure. A few bases in the west still have a *Tag der Offenen Tür* ('Open Door Day') but with little flying participation.

Luftwaffe aircraft are organised into a *Geschwader* (Wing) at each base. These usually have two *Staffeln* (Squadrons) each, although the wing badge is worn by all aircraft. For example, the second squadron of 31 Fighter-Bomber Wing would be expressed as 2/JBG 31 or 2/JaBoG 31 in the traditional German form, or as No 312 Squadron in the NATO system. Wing numbers indicate the role (50-series for reconnaissance; 70-series for interceptors; etc), so when the aircraft at a base change function, their badge remains the same. In an extreme case, JG 72, AG 54, LKG 43 and JBG 43 are successive identities linked to a single badge, but — to make life more interesting — the current JG 72 has the old JBG 36 insignia.

Most air bases in the far west were built for NATO in the 1950s and are functional, if lacking character. In the centre and south will be found a higher proportion of installations dating from before 1945. One such example, recently vacated, was RAF Gütersloh, where a large early 1980s hangar rubbed shoulders with 1970s HASs and traditional-style 1930s accommodation blocks and messes, the last-mentioned complete with anecdotes of Hermann Goering's visits. The army helicopter base at Fritzlar was feared by Allied bomber crews as a major night-fighter base and Peenemünde was birthplace of the V-1 and V-2 weapons.

Postwar, many bases have had more than one nation in residence. The move-ment of NATO forces to new bases in the far west coincided with rebirth of the *Luftwaffe* on 24 September 1956 and allowed the new force to occupy some recently vacated airfields. Ten years later, France's withdrawal from NATO brought about more switches of base as Söllingen, Lahr, Zweibrucken and Bremgarten changed hands.

Rebuilding of the *Luftwaffe* was accomplished rapidly over some five years, mostly with aircraft of diminishing effectiveness which happened to be available at the time: F/RF-84F Thunderstreaks/flashes; Canadian and Italian-built F-86 Sabres; and Nord Noratlases for transport. During the 1960s, Lockheed F-104G Starfighters and Fiat G.91Rs equipped the front line, whilst the 1970s saw McDonnell Douglas F-4 Phantoms shoulder some of the responsibility and Transall C.160Ds become the standard medium-sized transport. In the present decade, Panavia's Tornado is the main attack aircraft, its lighter companion, the Alpha Jet A, having suffered an abbreviated career.

Naval aviation, the *Marineflieger*, has progressed from Hawker Sea Hawks through Starfighters to Tornados — half of which were passed to the air force in 1993. Still in service are the Atlantics which replaced the first-generation maritime patrol aircraft, the Fairey Gannet.

Heeresflieger, the army's air arm, is equipped entirely with helicopters, including a few of the Sud Alouette IIs received in the late 1950s. MBB PAH-1s (Bö105Ps) are the main anti-tank helicopter, supported by unarmed VBH (105M) versions for liaison and observation. Transport is the role of Bell UH-1D Iroquois and Sikorsky CH-53Gs — all locally built. Army helicopter regiments (HFR) normally comprise two *staffeln* at one base, perhaps doubled-up with an autonomous squadron (HFS).

BRÜGGEN

Location: 3¾ miles (6km) SE of Brüggen
ICAO code: EDUR
Runway: 09/27 (8,159ft/2,487m)

The RAF base in Germany least affected by recent force reductions, Brüggen continues to host four Tornado GR1 strike/attack squadrons in HAS sites. These are No IX (badge: a bat), No 14 (winged disc), No 17 (red gauntlet) and No 31 (a star), making Brüggen the RAF's most potent base. The Army Air Corps is represented by 12 Flight with four Gazelles. Glider flying at weekends by the RAFGSA.

A minor road from An der Wae degenerates into a track which passes south of the 27 threshold, but this may be affected

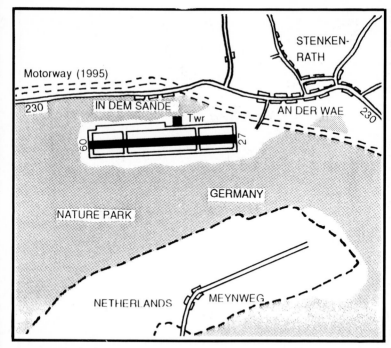

by motorway construction. Access from other directions is difficult or impossible.

RAF Brüggen was carved out of forest and marshland in under 12 months and occupied from 25 May 1953 onwards. Vampire FB5s of Nos 112 and 130 Sqn arrived on 6 June and 1 August 1953, but gave way to Sabres in January 1954. Two more Sabre squadrons, Nos 67 and 71, joined the wing in July 1955, all four converting to Hunter F4s early in 1956 and then disbanding between April and July 1957. From attack, Brüggen moved to a mixture of roles. No 80 Sqn arrived with Canberra PR.7s on 11 June 1957; No 87 with Meteor NF11s on 2 July 1957 (Javelins from November); and No 213 with the RAF's only Canberra B(I)6s on 22 August 1957. The fighter role vanished with disbandment of No 87 in January 1961, but the two Canberra squadrons remained until the end of 1969.

Nuclear strike and attack was the station's next — and current — function. Nos 14 and 17 Sqn were installed on 30 June and 16 October 1970 with Phantom FGR2s, and No 2 was briefly resident in 1970-71. No 31 joined them on 20 July 1971. The first Jaguar GR1 arrived for No 14 on 9 April 1975 and the base housed four Jaguar units with the formation of No 20 on 1 March 1977. In June 1984, No 31 moved up to Tornados and though No 20 was lost in June 1984, its place was taken by No IX from the UK on 1 October 1986.

BÜCHEL

Location: Between Büchel and Alflen villages
ICAO code: EDSB
Runway: 04/22 8,225ft/2,507m)

Jagdbombergeschwader (JBG) 33 is based here in the strike/attack role with two squadrons of Tornado IDS interdictors. A technical training unit, the *Lehrwerkstatt* has a few F-104 and G.91 instructional airframes and there are F-104s preserved on the gate and associated housing estate.

There are three HAS sites at Büchel: two in the south and one in the northwest.

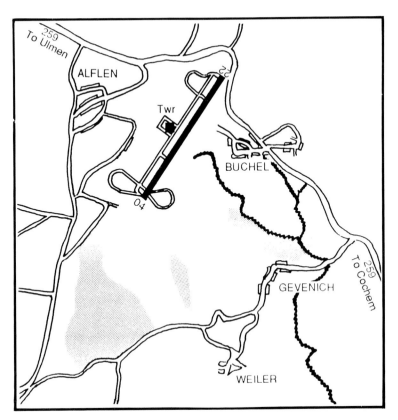

Panoramic views of the base are available from a shrine on a hillside immediately north of Büchel village. The 22 approach is accessible from waste ground on the north side of the 259 road, but this is below airfield level. To the west of the field, a track originates from the road at the 04 approach and leads around the southeast loop.

Büchel was transferred to the *Luftwaffe* on 8 December 1955. *Waffenschule* 30 moved in from Fürstenfeldbruck in July 1957 as the training unit for F-84F Thunderstreak wings, its first task being the formation of JBG 31 on 1 September 1957. That wing moved to Nörvenich on 20 January 1958 to complete working-up and on 2 July 1958 WS 30 passed its training commitment to WS 50 at Erding and became an operational wing, JBG 33. Starfighters re-equipped JBG 33 from

August 1962 until the last sortie was flown on 30 May 1985 and the first Tornado was received in August 1985.

EGGEBEK
Location: 1½ miles (3km) W of Eggebek
ICAO code: EDCG
Runway: 01/19 (8,005ft/2,440m)

Two Tornado IDS squadrons now constitute naval aviation's attack and reconnaissance force, both operating from Eggebek as *Marinefliegergeschwader* 2. The recce role is performed with a centreline pod on some aircraft of 1 *Aufklärungsstaffel*, whilst 2 *Mehrzweckstaffel* is assigned to anti-shipping missions.

Roads on the north, east and south provide good views of activity on this flat airfield.

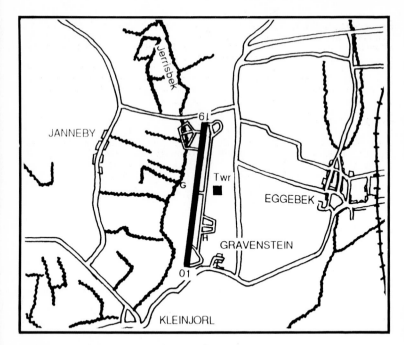

Rebuilt after World War 2, Eggebek began its second lease of life as a *Luftwaffe* base, receiving the RF-84F Thunderflashes of AG 52 from Erding in November 1960. The wing moved out to nearby Leck in October 1964 to receive RF-104G Starfighters and was replaced in March 1965 by MFG 2, which immediately began receiving Starfighters, including one squadron of RF-104Gs. MFG 2 took delivery of its first Tornado on 11 September 1986 and flew the last F-104 sortie in May 1987. A regular feature of its operations was the daily 'Eastern Express' reconnaissance flight over the Baltic to plot shipping off the east German and Polish coasts.

GEILENKIRCHEN

Location: 3 miles (5km) W of
    Geilenkirchen
ICAO code: EDNG
Runway: 09/27 (10,009ft/3,050m)
A truly international air base, Geilenkirchen is headquarters of the NATO Airborne Early Warning Force's E-3A Component. Not all 18 Sentries will be found operating from here simultaneously, for the NAEWF has regular detachments to Konya (Turkey), Previza (Greece), Trapani (Italy) and Ørland (Norway). At the time of writing, aircraft at Trapani and Previza were involved in policing the Bosnian 'No Fly' zone — the NAEWF's first operational commitment. All duties are shared with the RAF element of seven E-3Ds at Waddington. Additionally resident are three ex-airline Boeing 707-329Cs which are used for training flightdeck crew and carrying support equipment. The 21 aircraft wear the national markings of Luxembourg. Pairs of Air National Guard KC-135 tankers are based here to support the E-3 force.

Both ends of the runway are accessible, but the road to the east is additionally useful for viewing the ramps.

Geilenkirchen, Brüggen, Laarbruch and Wildenrath were built for the RAF in the early 1950s and collectively known as the 'Clutch' bases. When opened, Geilenkirchen had an 8,100ft (2,469m) runway and was assigned to fighter-bomber and reconnaissance tasks. The Sabres of No 3

Sqn were posted-in on 20 June 1953 and augmented by No 234 on 8 January 1954, both converting to Hunters early in 1956 before disbanding on 15 June 1957. No 2 Sqn arrived for recce with Meteor FR9s on 25 October 1955, swiftly changed to Swift FR5s three months later, then left for Jever in October 1957.

Canberra B(I)8s of No 59 Sqn arrived as replacements the following month and stayed until February 1961, by which time Geilenkirchen was also in the air defence world. Meteor NF11s of Nos 96 and 256 Sqn were resident for 11 months from 12 February 1958 before they were renumbered as Nos 3 and 11 Sqn and moved-up to Javelins.

When No 3 disbanded on 1 January 1961, No 59 was renumbered to continue the tradition and the B(I)8s stayed at Geilenkirchen for another seven years as part of RAF Germany's NATO-assigned tactical nuclear strike force. Both Javelin units stood-down late in 1965 to be replaced by the Lightning F2s of No 92

Sqn on 29 December 1965. It was soon decided to concentrate the RAFG Lightning force at Wildenrath and No 92 moved out in January 1968, together with No 3.

Geilenkirchen passed into German hands and was used as the HQ of a SAM missile wing. When the NAEWF treaty was signed on 6 December 1978 the station was nominated for extensive rebuilding as the main operating base. The first E-3A was delivered on 24 February 1982 and on 28 June that year the NAEWF was inaugurated and Geilenkirchen handed-over to NATO control. The first 707TCA (Trainer/Cargo Aircraft) was accepted on 26 April 1989. Deployments of ANG KC-135s began on 11 January 1993.

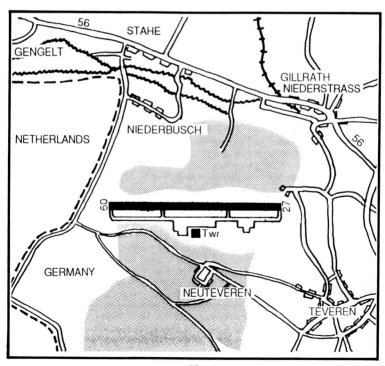

Vanishing sights. East German Sukhoi Su-22 'Fitters' have not been incorporated into the post-unification *Luftwaffe*, but their base at Laage is to house a Phantom and 'Fulcrum' interceptor wing. It is interesting to compare the ex-Soviet Bloc style of HAS with its Western equivalent. *Peter Foster*

A snowy day at Schleswig. Armed with Kormoran anti-ship missiles beneath the fuselage, a Tornado is directed to its shelter. These aircraft have now been transferred to the *Luftwaffe*. *Panavia*

A rare sight at Nordholz is the 'Peace Peek' modification of Atlantic for ELINT duties. The fixed ventral radome, positioned well forward, is a recognition feature. *via Paul Jackson*

Earmarked for retirement like their extinct *Luftwaffe* brethren are Dornier 28D Skyservants of MFG5. *Paul Jackson*

JBG32's force of ECM Hansa Jets has been reduced from seven to three. *Paul Jackson*

HOHN

Location: 1¾ miles (3km) NE of Hohn
ICAO code: EDNQ
Runway: 08/26 (8,005ft/2,440m)

Hohn caters for fixed and rotary-wing transport requirements, with two squadrons of Transall C.160Ds and one of UH-1D Iroquois in residence with *Lufttransportgeschwader* 62. The UH-1s have a secondary SAR role in view of the proximity of Hohn to the North Sea and Baltic.

South side of the runway can be monitored at each end from either the blocked road on the eastern edge of the large wood (from where a track passes under the 26 approach) or from a track originating immediately north of Hohn village and skirting the western edge of the wood. The track just north of the main gate is also useful.

One of Germany's 'newest' airfields — although built on the site of an abandoned World War 2 base — Hohn received its first major unit when the Noratlases of LTG 63 arrived from Celle on 1 December 1967. C.160s were delivered in as replacements from 26 April 1968 and equipped both squadrons, the last 'Nora' departing in March 1971. With the running-down of HTG 64, a *staffel* (2/64) of UH-1Ds was transferred from Ahlhorn in June 1993 as 3/HTG 63. Hohn was also the base of target-facilities Fiat G.91s flown by Condor Flugdienst until the last departed the base on 28 January 1993 for museum preservation.

HOLZDORF

Location: Immediately SE of Holzdorf
ICAO code: n/k
Runway: 09/27 (7,710ft/2,350m)

A more even distribution of *Luftwaffe*

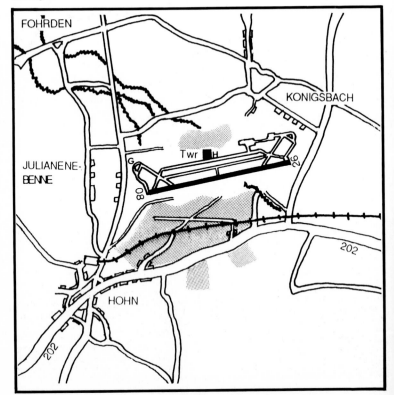

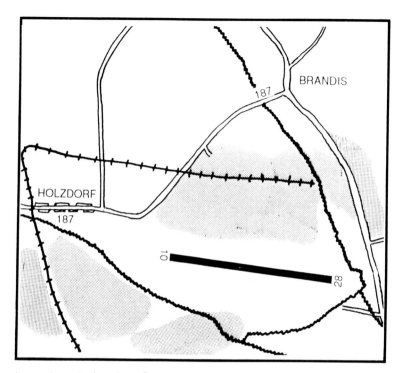

transport assets throughout Germany is being achieved by transfer of LTG 62 from Wunsdorf. On 1 October 1993, a UH-1D detachment was formed at the base with helicopters transferred from the disbanding HTG 64 to LTG 62. Hoizdorf will receive 24 UH-1s of the newly-formed 3/LTG 62, but relocation of the two Transall C.160D squadrons will be delayed for some time due to inadequate infrastructure at the base and will not be complete until 2002.

Aircraft approaching Runway 27 can be seen from a short, blocked road in the southeast corner of the map.

Built for the LSK/LV, Holzdorf was the home of *Jagdfliegergeschwader* 1 'Fritz Schmenkel' and its MiG-21MF 'Fishbeds' when Germany was unified in 1990. The wing ceased operation in October 1990 and its MiGs were moved to Drewitz, where they were scrapped in 1992-93.

HOPSTEN

Location: 3 miles (5km) SW of Hopsten
ICAO code: EDNP
Runway: 01/19 (8,005ft/2,440m)

Two squadrons of air defence F-4E/ICE Phantoms constitute *Jagdgeschwader* 72 'Westfalen' at Hopsten. A third element of the wing, the *Zentrale Ausbildungsstaffel* uses F-4s to give 'Europeanisation' conversion courses to personnel trained to operate the Phantom in the USA. Since July 1992, the wing has been equipped with the upgraded ICE (Improved Combat Efficiency) version, featuring AN/APG-65 pulse-Doppler radar and AIM-120 AMRAAM missiles.

Aircraft on the runway can be photographed from a track on the east side of the base, originating on the Drierwalde-Hörstel road.

The original Hopsten air base was built on a three-runway pattern in 1940 and saw operations by both Me262 and Ar234 jets before being captured by the Allies as airfield B112 and briefly hosting an RAF

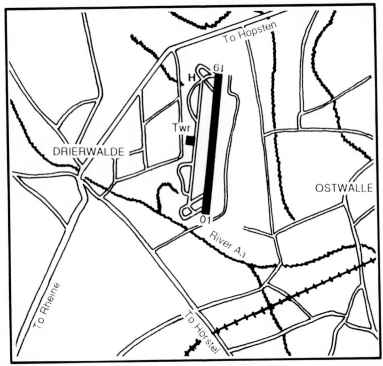

Tempest/Typhoon wing in the closing days of the war. A new aerodrome was built in 1960 and received its first occupant when the half-formed JBG 36 flew its F-84Fs in from Nörvenich on 21 August 1961. The wing (still with only one squadron) was declared operational on 12 December and formed a second component in the following month. Still in the fighter-bomber role, JBG 36 received its first F-104G Starfighter on 2 February 1965, then converted to Phantoms from April 1975. After assuming a 40% air defence commitment, the wing turned totally to fighter operations on 1 November 1990 when it was redesignated JG 72.

JEVER

Location: 2½ miles (4km) S of Jever
ICAO code: EDNJ
Runway: 10/28 (8,136ft/2,480m)

Aircrew who have converted to flying the Tornado IDS at RAF Cottesmore learn how to use its weapon system at Jever before being posted to an operational squadron. The 1st *Staffel* of *Jagdbombergeschwader* 38 'Friesland' is the OCU and has a high proportion of dual control Tornados. It is partnered by a second squadron with an operational tasking — originally ECM and reconnaissance, but strike/attack from July 1994. The Phantom overhaul unit, *Luftwaffenwerft* 62 is another resident.

Both ends of the runway can be viewed from blocked roads in the southeast and under the western approach. Jever's long history began with its opening on 1 May 1936. It became Allied airfield B117 and postwar the RAF laid a concrete runway in 1948, although no squadrons were based at the site until the NATO expansion of the early 1950s. A Vampire fighter-bomber wing (Nos 4, 93 and 112 Sqn) was installed in March 1952 and, although No 112 left in July 1953, the other two units remained until December 1960 and progressed through Sabres

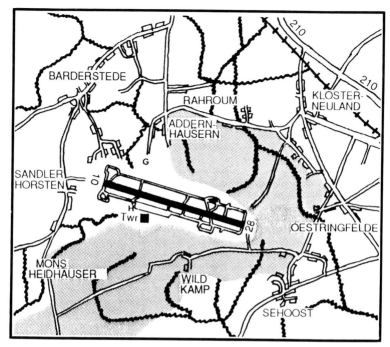

(1954) and Hunters (1956), augmented between spring 1955 and summer 1957 by the Hunters of Nos 98 and 118. No 2 Sqn arrived with Swift FR5s in October 1957 and had just converted to Hunter FR10s when it departed in October 1961 and the base was turned over to the *Luftwaffe*.

After further runway rebuilding and extensive infrastructure changes, the Starfighter OCU, *Waffenschule* 10 arrived from Nörvenich on 7 February 1964, bringing F-104Gs and a sizeable number of two-seat F-104Fs and TF-104Gs. Activities were wound down early in 1983 and on 26 August that year the unit was transformed into JBG 38 with the Tornados formerly used by the *Waffenausbildungskomponent* at Erding. The second squadron was added in 1990 when deliveries began of the Tornado ECR and the only other ECR squadron, 1/JBG 32, trained at Jever before deployment. Following a decision to concentrate the ECR force at Lechfeld, 2/JBG 38 swapped its aircraft for the standard IDS Tornados of 2/JBG 32 in July 1994.

LAAGE

Location: 1¾ miles (3km) WSW of Laage
ICAO code: n/k
Runway: 10/28 (7,874ft/2,400m)

Sole air defence base in the former East Germany, Laage gained a detachment of F-4E Phantoms from 35 Wing on 1 October 1993 and is to be fully reactivated on 1 October 1994 with the arrival of *Jagdgeschwader* 73 from Preschen with MiG-29 'Fulcrums'. Uniquely for the *Luftwaffe*, JG 73 is a mixed-type fighter wing with one squadron of MiGs and one of F-4F Phantoms — the latter provided through the disbandment of JG 35 at Husum.

Laage was most recently East Germany's sole base for Su-22M-4 'Fitter' attack aircraft. *Jagdbombenfliegergeschwader* 77 'Gebhard Leberecht von Blücher' was established in 1984 and in the following year, a naval wing, *Marinefliegergeschwader* 28 'Paul Wieczorek' was added. Despite the newness of the aircraft, they were not retained after unification and were placed in storage in the

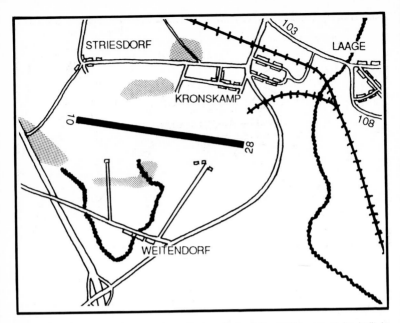

STRIESDORF

KRONSKAMP

LAAGE

103

108

10

28

WEITENDORF

HAS and maintenance areas (mostly north of the runway) at Laage prior to scrapping.

LAARBRUCH

Location: 3 miles (5km) SW of Weeze
ICAO code: EDUL
Runway: 09/27 (8,012ft/2,442m)

Long associated with strike/attack, Laarbruch is now dedicated to support of the British Army in Germany. Fixed-wing assets comprise the Harrier GR7s of No 3 Sqn (cockatrice badge and AA-AZ codes) and No IV Sqn (lightning flash; CA-CZ). A mixed helicopter support squadron, No 18 (Pegasus; BA-BZ), has five Pumas and five Chinooks as well as a Gazelle on loan from No 2 FTS. Consideration has been given to withdrawing the Harriers to the UK. Weekend glider flying by the RAFGSA.

There is a vantage point on the east side of the road, north of the 27 approach. Disued roads at the 09 end give access to that approach and — if not obstructed by extensions to the airfield — pass by the northwest HAS site to the St Petrushm-Hees road.

Last of the RAF bases to be built in Germany, Laarbruch was constructed in a forest and received the Canberra PR3s (later PR7s) of No 69 Sqn on 5 May 1954. No 79's Meteor FR9s, No 541's Meteor PR10s and the F-84E Thunderjets of Netherlands No 306 Sqn followed in November and the recce wing was completed by No 31 squadron, formed on 1 March 1955 with Canberra PR7s and the similarly-equipped No 80 on 20 June that year. No 217, also with PR7s, stayed at Laarbruch for a couple of months in mid-1955.

The Meteor left the station in November 1955, only to return in night-fighter guise when the NF11s of No 68 Sqn were installed in January 1957. Defence cuts resulted in departure of two PR7 squadrons — No 80 in June 1957 and No 69 in July 1958 — but No 31 remained unchanged until the end of March 1971. The Dutch contingent had exchanged its camera-equipped F-84Es for RF-84F Thunderflashes from 4 April 1956 onwards, but moved to Deelen in December 1957. Laarbruch's interceptor squadron was transformed by renumbering as No 5 Sqn on 20 January 1959 and began the change to Javelins before mov-

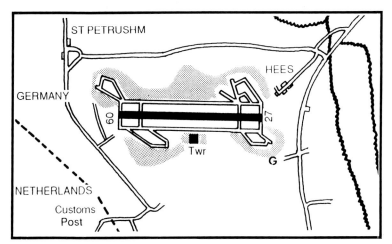

ing out to Geilenkirchen in December 1962.

Reorientation of the station to strike/attack began when the Canberra B(I)8s of No 16 Sqn arrived on 1 March 1958. No 3 moved in a decade later, but both disbanded during the first half of 1972. By way of replacement, Laarbruch became the home of the RAF's overseas Buccaneer force when Nos XV and 16 Sqn arrived in January 1971 and October 1972. In the recce role, departure of Canberra PR7s was rectified by No II Sqn's Phantoms, installed on 23 May 1971 and supplanted by Jaguars in 1976 and Tornados in 1988.

By then, Laarbruch was a Tornado strike/attack base, having converted Nos XV and 16 in 1983-84 and added No 20 in June 1984. The wing of four Tornado squadrons lasted only until 1992: No II transferred to the UK in December 1991 and the remaining three units disbanded between September 1991 and July 1992. The residents of RAF Gütersloh were moved west to Laarbruch to fill their places, beginning with Nos 3 and IV Sqn on 16 and 27 November 1992 and ending with No 18 on 17 March 1993.

LECHFELD

Location: 3 miles (5km) NE of Klosterlechfeld
ICAO code: EDSL
Runway: 03/21 (8,012ft/2,442m)

Main unit at Lechfeld is *Jagdbombergeschwader* 32 with two squadrons of Tornado ECRs in the electronic combat and reconnaissance roles and one squadron (3/32) of seven HFB 320ECM Hansas and a single Antonov An-26SM providing electronic warfare training. The latter's former navaids calibration task is performed by the *Gemeinsame Flugmessungsstaffel* with civilian-registered BAe 125s and 748s.

Both approaches can be photographed from minor roads, but views of other areas are difficult because of military camps bordering the Landsberg-Augsburg highway and a river and woods to the east. Several preserved aircraft are located at various points of the large Lechfeld military complex.

The second of the new *Luftwaffe*'s attack wings, JBG 32, formed at Lechfeld on 22 July 1958 flying F-84F Thunderstreaks and remained thus equipped until the first F-104G Starfighter was received on the final day of 1964. This aircraft flew its final operation on 18 April 1984, prior to Tornado IDS deliveries beginning on 27 July 1984. During 1991, 1/32 *Staffel* converted to Tornado ECRs at Jever and the wing gained a second squadron with the same variant when 2/32 made a direct swap of aircraft with 2/38 at Jever in July 1994. JBG 32 is the only one of the four Tornado attack wings (31-34) not to have nuclear weapons.

Fernmelde Lehr und Versuchsregiment 61 (Radar Training and Research Regi-

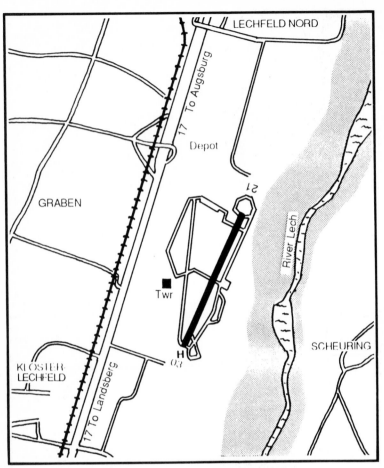

ment) formed at Ulrichs Kaserne, Lechfeld North on 23 March 1961 and added *Flugvermessungstaffel* 4/61 at Lechfeld on 30 May 1964 with a calibration and radar/ECM training fleet of Pembrokes, Do27s, C-47s and Noratlases from Nörvenich. The calibration element was civilianised when the C-47s were withdrawn on 14 April 1976 and on 31 August that year the first of eight Hansas arrived following installation of jamming equipment. *Staffel* 4/61 became 3/32 on 1 April 1980.

MEMMINGEN

Location: 2½ miles (4km) ESE of Memmingen
ICAO code: EDSM
Runway: 06/24 (7,874ft/2,400m)

Jagdbombergeschwader 34 'Allgäu', the last wing to re-equip with Tornados, is based at Memmingen with two squadrons. Duties are strike and attack with weapons including B61 nuclear bombs held by the USA.

Proceedings may be viewed from tracks on the north side of the airfield which run eastwards past the tower. The 24 approach is also accessible from the

Ungerhausen-Hawangen road. Hangars and ramp can be seen from the Benningen-Hawangen road.

In the new *Luftwaffe*'s early days, Memmingen acted as a base depot from which several training units were formed, all of them elements of *Flugzeugführerschule* 'S'. FFS-S moved in from Uetersen on 4 August 1956 and then detached the primary training element (Super Cubs and P.149Ds of *Ausbildungsstaffel* A) to Diepholz in March 1958. The transport training component (Ausb-Stf B) with C-47s and Noratlases moved to Neubiberg at the same time and Bell 47Gs and Vertol H-21s of AusbStf C were despatched to Fassberg in October 1958. In the opposite direction, JBG 34, which had formed at Fassberg in November 1958 came to Memmingen on 11 April 1959 with its F-84F Thunderstreaks and was declared operational on 5 May.

The first F-104G Starfighter arrived on 1 July 1964 and conversion of the two squadrons was completed in May 1966. JBG 34 took over the residual F-104 training commitment in 1983 after WS-10 converted to Tornados and accordingly gained an extra allocation of TF-104Gs. At length, its final Starfighter sortie was flown on 16 October 1987 and conversion to Tornados began immediately thereafter. The wing was operational again in June 1988 and was awarded the name 'Allgäu' on 8 May 1992.

NEUBURG
Location: 2½ miles (4km) SE of Neuburg
ICAO code: EDSU
Runway: 09/27 (8,005ft/2,440m)
Like its long-term northern counterpart at Wittmund, resident air defence wing, *Jagdgeschwader* 74 'Molders' was unable to undertake peacetime policing of German airspace because of treaty restrictions and left the task to RAF and USAF interceptors. That has changed since unification in October 1990. Not only do both wings have the improved F-4E/ICE Phantom, they were also given the additional assignment in 1993 of supporting units for NATO's Rapid Reaction Force.

Not to be confused with Neubiberg, this base is open to observation from

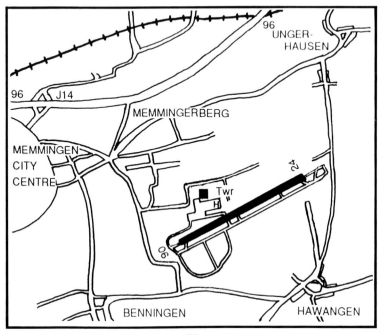

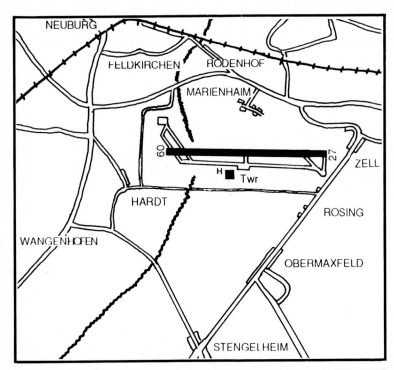

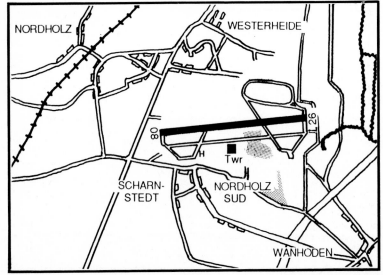

66

most points. Of greatest value are tracks originating at Hardt and progressing eastwards to Rosing and northwards under the 09 approach.

Neuburg's operational career began on 1 May 1961 when JG 75 arrived from Leipheim with its F-86K Sabre all-weather fighters and immediately became JG 74. Upgrading to F-104G Starfighters began with the first delivery on 12 May 1964 and was complete by the end of 1965. The name of World War 2 air ace, Werner Molders was bestowed on the wing on 3 November 1973. After flying its last F-104 sortie on 30 June 1974, JG 74 began receiving F-4E Phantoms and returned to combat readiness in May 1976.

NORDHOLZ

Location: Immediately SE of Nordholz
ICAO code: EDCN
Runway: 08/26 (8,002ft/2,439m)

One of only two operational naval air bases remaining, Nordholz is home to *Marinefliegergeschwader* 3 and its three component squadrons. The first two fly Germany's fleet of Atlantic maritime patrol aircraft, but whilst 1 *Ubterseeboote Jagdstaffel* undertakes straightforward anti-submarine work, 2 *Unterseeboote Jagd und Aufklärungsstaffel* has an additional reconnaissance tasking. The latter, in fact, refers to the five Atlantics modified for ELINT work with a large, black radome protruding from the sealed weapons bay. Finally, 3 *Hubschrauberstaffel* is equipped with Lynx for operations from the rear decks of 'Bremen' class frigates of the *Bundesmarine*.

Built on the flat land of northern Germany, Nordholz is reasonably open to outside inspection and photography of aircraft on the approach. Short tracks lead to the northwest, southwest and southeast extremities of the runway.

First operational units at newly-completed Nordholz were the Sea Hawk fighter-bombers of 1/ and 2/MFG 2 which arrived from Schleswig in April 1963 and moved out to Eggebek in March 1965. By then, however, there had been a change of emphasis, as MFG 3 was established on 1 July 1964 with the transfer at Westerland-Sylt of Gannet AS4s formerly of 3/MFG 2. The squadron moved into Nord-

holz on 1 December that year. A second *staffel* (actually 1/MFG 3) formed in December 1965 to receive Atlantics allowing the last Gannets to be withdrawn in October 1966. With the advent of frigate-operated helicopters, 3 *Staffel* formed in June 1971 and installed its first seagoing detachment on the GNS *Bremen* in July 1982.

NÖRVENICH

Location: 1¾ miles (3km) NNE of Nörvenich
ICAO code: EDNN
Runway: 07/25 (8,005ft/2,440m)

Germany's premier strike/attack wing is based at Nörvenich in the form of *Jagdbombergeschwader* 31 'Boelcke', operating two squadrons of Tornados. The *Luftwaffe* planned to form a new helicopter squadron at the base in April 1994, equipped with 20 UH-1D Iroquois.

Flugplatz Nörvenich is largely shrouded in trees, but both approaches can be observed from the public roads at each end of the runway. Additionally, a track runs to the southeast corner of the airfield from the Onnau-Rath road.

One of the *Luftwaffe*'s first operational bases following re-formation, Nörvenich opened on 1 April 1957 with formation of *Waffenschule* 10, equipped with Sabres. This transferred to Oldenburg a few months later and was replaced on 20 January 1958 by the recently-established JBG 31 from Büchel. Equipped with F-84F Thunderstreaks, the wing became operational on 20 June 1958 as the first front-line unit of the re-formed *Luftwaffe* and in January 1959 it again made history when assigned to NATO.

WS-10 returned to Nörvenich in July 1960 after the base was chosen to be the first with Starfighters. Named for fighter ace, Ernst Boelcke on 21 April 1961, JBG 31 then started Starfighter conversion, returning to operational status on 20 February 1962. WS-10 transferred to Jever in February 1964. At length, JBG 31 stood down on 30 April 1983 and received its first Tornado on 26 July, the transition lasting a year. The wing also ushered into service the MW-1 belly-mounted weapons dispenser, of which deliveries were made to Nörvenich on 22 November 1984. As the *Luftwaffe*'s

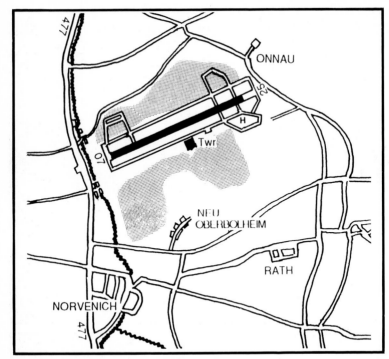

first combat-rated Tornado base, Nörvenich despatched the aircraft on its first German-manned participation in 'Red Flag' in November 1989, partnering JBG 32.

PRESCHEN

Location: 1¾ miles (3km) NW of Preschen
ICAO code: n/k
Runway: 07/25 (8,202ft/2,500m)

In October 1994, Preschen's sole residents — the MiG-29 'Fulcrum As' of JG 73 — will move north to Laage to continue their task of defending eastern Germany's airspace. Preschen is unlikely to be used for other purposes, as part of its circuit is over Poland.

There are HAS sites on all four corners of the airfield, those for the MiG-29s being close to the main ramp on the northwest side. Tracks from Jocksdorf lead to the western approach.

Then known as *Jagdfliegergeschwader* 3, the resident wing augmented its

MiG-21MF 'Fishbeds' with MiG-29s in 1988, equipping two squadrons with 24 aircraft, including four two-seat versions. These 'Fulcrums' were the only combat aircraft selected for continued service in the wake of German unification. JFG 3 was retitled as an experimental unit, *Erprobungsgeschwader* 29, regaining operational status on 1 June 1993 as *Jagdgeschwader* 73.

RAMSTEIN

Location: 2½ miles (4km) SE of Ramstein-Miesenbach
ICAO code: EDAR
Runway: 09/27 (8,031ft/2,448m)

Ramstein is HQ US Air Forces in Europe (USAFE); a major airhead for Air Mobility Command; a staging-post for aircraft deliveries (recently including Egyptian and Israeli F-16s); and base of the 86th Wing. The last-mentioned comprises the 37th

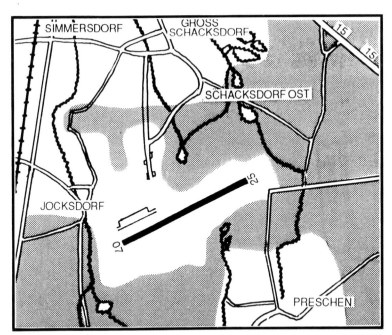

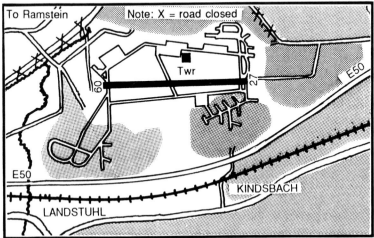

ALS (arriving 1994) for transport support with Hercules; 76th ALS, providing communications and light transport services to HQ USAFE with a mixed fleet of C-20A, C-21A and CT-43A; and the 75th AAS with C-9A Nightingales equipped for medical evacuation. Two squadrons of F-16Cs (512th and 526th) transferred to 31st FW at Aviano from April 1994.

Aircraft landing at the 09 end can be photographed from a track which runs south to the approach. The 27 end is reached by leaving the E50 motorway at Junction 14 and turning left on to a track shortly before the start of the prohibited road system. The *Bismarck Turm* (tower) in Landstuhl provides an elevated, if distant, view of activity at the base, but part of the visitors' ramp cannot be seen from even this vantage point.

Known until August 1958 as Landstuhl, the base received its first major unit when F-86E Sabres of the 86th FBW arrived from Neubiberg in July 1952. By April 1953, these were being replaced by the first F-86Fs to be stationed in Europe. To reflect the interception role, the 86th was designated a FIW in August 1954 and was considerably expanded when it absorbed two squadrons of Air Defense Command Sabres which had been co-located with the 7486th Air Defense Group. Re-equipment at Ramstein with F-102 Delta Daggers brought about a change of title to 86th Air Division in November 1959, the Division being responsible for detached squadrons at Soesterberg, Hahn and Bitburg. Ramstein's F-102 squadron, the 526th, became autonomous when the 86th disbanded on 14 November 1968, but it was absorbed into the 26th TRW on 1 November 1959.

On arrival from Toul, France, in October 1966, the 26th had but one squadron (38th) of RF-4C Phantoms. Its newly acquired interceptor element flew the final European F-102 operational sortie from Ramstein on 1 April 1970 before re-equipping with F-4Es. In a change-round of USAFE units effective from 31 January 1973, the RF-4s and 26th TRW went to Zweibrucken, from where the re-formed 86th TFW arrived to take over the 526th. It remained a one-squadron wing until the 512th was added on 15 November 1976. The F-4Es were replaced by F-16Cs from September 1985, whilst newer (Block 40) versions of the latter were substituted in 1993-94 prior to the two fighter squadrons moving out to form the 31st FW at Aviano, Italy.

Other notable units resident at Ramstein in the past have included nuclear-armed F-86F Sabres and F-100C Super Sabres of the 461st FDS on detachment from Bitburg; C-123B Providers and (from 27 February 1968) C-130E-I Hercules of the 7th Air Commando Squadron/7th SOS; Cessna O-2As of 601st TCW (detached from Wiesbaden in 1970-73); and the HQ wing for European-based

HH-43 Huskies, the 40th ARRW, which disbanded on 30 June 1973. USAFE HQ moved in during 1972. Recent changes have included withdrawal of C-12Fs (on 23 September 1993) and UH-1Ns from the former 58th ALS shortly before its re-designation as the 76th on 1 October 1993 and simultaneous renaming of the former 55th AAS (which arrived from Rhein-Main with its C-9As in July 1993) as 75th AAS. Departure of F-16s and their replacement by the 37th ALS Hercules from Rhein-Main was due for Fiscal Year (FY) 1994.

SCHLESWIG-JAGEL

Location: 1 mile (2km) W of Jagel
ICAO code: EDCS
Runways: 05/23 (8,005ft/2,440m); 08/26 (6,873ft/2,095m)

Since 1 January 1994, Schleswig-Jagel has been a *Luftwaffe* base, following its take over of 40 Tornados formerly belonging to naval air wing MFG 1. These are now tasked with reconnaissance under *Aufklärungsgeschwader* 51, but only nine centreline recce pods have been acquired — six of them from Italy. A requirement has been issued for a comprehensive recce kit for AG 51, although it will be several years before it is available.

The roads from Jagel to Mielberg to Kleine Rhede give good views over the airfield. The north side can be reached by a road running south from a crossroads 2 miles (3km) northeast of Kleine Rhede.

Between July and September 1945, seven RAF Spitfire, Typhoon or Tempest squadrons (Nos 26, 56, 175, 181, 182, 184 and 245) passed through the old *Luftwaffe* base at Schleswigland (Allied airfield B164), of which Nos 181 and 182 (Typhoons) disbanded there on 30 September. On 1 November 1948, the newly-delivered Hastings C1s of No 47 Sqn deployed to Schleswigland to participate in the Berlin Airlift and were augmented by No 297's aircraft from 13 December. No 53 Sqn replaced No 47 in mid-1949 and the detachment ended when No 297 returned to the UK on 7 October that year.

Rebuilt for the *Marineflieger*, the renamed Schleswig-Jagel was the home of MFG 1 when it formed on 2 March 1957. After training in the UK, the first component squadron of Sea Hawks

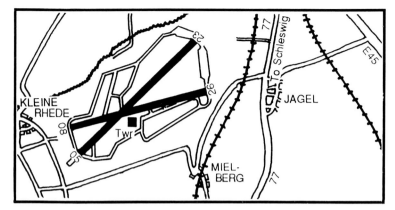

arrived at Jagel on 20 June 1958, closely followed by a Gannet squadron. On 1 July 1958, MFG 2 was established with Sea Hawks, gaining the Gannets in October 1961, but deploying them to Westerland-Sylt in February 1962. MFG 2 transferred to Nordholz in April 1963 and MFG 1 took delivery of its first F-104G Starfighter on 19 September 1963.

The wing flew its final F-104 mission on 29 October 1981 and stood down for Tornado conversion, receiving its initial aircraft on 2 July 1982 and becoming operational as the first German unit with the Tornado on 1 January 1984. More recently, following the down-declaration of RF-4E Phantom wing AG 51 at Bremgarten in September 1992 (it formally disbanded on 1 April 1993) *Luftwaffe Tornado Geschwader Jagel* was established on 1 January 1993 to convert crews on to the naval aircraft. The unit became *Luftwaffe Jagel* on 1 May that year prior to AG 51 being officially reborn on 1 January 1994, employing the panther badge of the old AG 52.

SPANGDAHLEM

Location: Immediately E of Spangdahlem
ICAO code: EDAD
Runway: 05/23 (10,000ft/6,214m)

Four squadrons of SP-coded fighter-bombers are based at Spangdahlem with the 52nd FW, including two with F-16Cs: 22nd FS (red fin stripe) and 23rd FS (blue). The wing is completed by one squadron of F-15C Eagles, the 53rd FS 'Tigers' (yellow/black) whilst Europe's last

A-10A Thunderbolts are operated by the 81st FS (yellow). Formerly equipped with F-4Gs (and then known as the 81st FS), the 22nd has 'Block 50D' F-16Cs optimised for carrying AGM-88 HARM anti-radar missiles in the 'Wild Weasel' defence-suppression role.

Aircraft landing on Runway 05 can be seen from the road linking Binfeld with the twin villages of Spang and Dahlem. The 23 approach can be reached by a track originating northeast of Dahlem. A track near Binfeld approaches the southern side of the runway, whilst an overall view can be obtained from west of Spang, on the road to Dudeldorf.

Spangdahlem began operations in May 1953 when RF-80 Shooting Stars and RB-26 Invaders of the 10th TRW moved in from Toul, France. The base's reconnaissance equipment was upgraded throughout the 1950s with RB-57 Canberras (1954), RF-84F Thunderflashes (1955) and RB-66 Destroyers (1956) before the 10th departed for Alconbury in August 1959. Its place was taken by the nuclear-capable F-100 Super Sabres of the 49th TFW which had been requested to leave France (with the similarly-armed 48th and 50th TFWs). Between 1961 and 1967, the resident 7th, 8th and 9th TFSs constituted Europe's only wing of F-105 Thunderchiefs, following which the 49th enjoyed a brief period with F-4D Phantoms before being recalled to the USA in June 1968 as an economy measure.

The Destroyer returned to 'Spang' in EB-66 guise when the 39th Tactical Electronic Warfare Squadron formed on 1 April 1969. Nearby Bitburg installed its

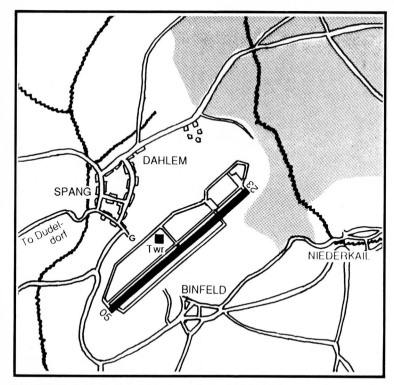

23rd TFS (F-4D Phantom) to take advantage of the part-empty facilities, both these units being absorbed into the 52nd TFW when it formed on 31 December 1971. The RB-66s lasted only until 1 January 1973 and were replaced a fortnight later by a new F-4C squadron from Zweibrucken, the 81st TFS. The 480th TFS (F-4D) was added in 1976 and all three squadrons received a mixture of F-4Es and 'Wild Weasel' F-4Gs in the defence-suppression role from 1979. F-4Es were replaced by F-16C Fighting Falcons in 1987 and the F-4Gs were partly withdrawn during 1991, leaving the 81st reorganised as the last USAFE Phantom operator.

During 1993 there were many changes at Spangdahlem, beginning on 4 January with official installation of the 510th FS from the UK with A-10As. The 81st began receiving F-16C-30s in February, initiating the Phantom's run-down, whilst Block 50 aircraft were supplied to the remaining two Fighting Falcon squadrons, starting the same month. The 'Wild Weasel' Block 50D version was following in FY 1994 for the 81st, but the process was overtaken by a complicated reorganisation early that year. This involved addition of F-15C Eagles of 53rd FS from the disbanding 36th FW at nearby Bitburg; disbandment of 480th and 510th FSs; re-formation of 22nd FS (from Bitburg) with 81st FS F-16s; and re-equipment of 81st FS with the A-10As.

WITTMUND

Location: 5½ miles (9km) WSW of Wittmund
ICAO code: EDNT
Runway: 08/26 (8,005ft/2,440m)
Resident wing at Wittmund is *Jabogeschwader* 71 'Richthofen', an air defence unit with two squadrons of F-4F/ICE Phantoms.

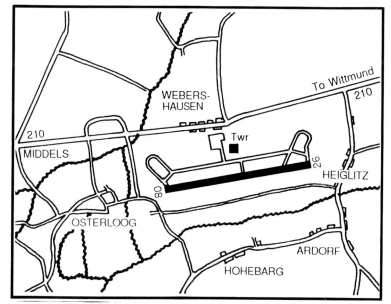

Flat, open land allows good views of the base. Landing aircraft can be seen from public roads at both ends of the runway. A track from Osterloog to Heiglitz runs along the south side of the base.

Wittmundhafen — as it was then known — received its first and only resident wing when JG 71 arrived from Ahlhorn with its Sabres in April 1963. Conversion to Starfighters began immediately and during the process a Sabre squadron was maintained at Oldenburg to meet NATO commitments. Replacement by F-4F Phantoms started with delivery of the first aircraft on 7 March 1974 and the Richthofen wing was redeclared combat-ready on 1 July 1975. Now upgraded to ICE standard with AIM-120 AMRAAM missiles, the Phantoms have been dedicated to NATO's Rapid Reaction force since 1993.

OTHER AIR FORCE AND GERMAN ARMY BASES:

In view of the many recent changes in air arm structures in Germany over the past few years, recently-closed bases are included in this list. 'Closed' is taken to mean an absence of significant military flying units, as some airfields, notably in the west, may still have ground elements resident or have been transferred to civil aviation.

- ● **Ahlhorn** Closed. Ex-HTG 64 (UH-1D).
- ● **Allstedt** Closed. Ex-294 Rgt (Su-17R); 225 Rgt (Mi-8, Mi-24).
- ● **Altenburg** Closed. Ex-968 Rgt (MiG-29).
- ● **Basepohl** 1¾ miles (3km) N of Reuterstadt Stavenhagen. HFS 30 (UH-1D). Ex-KHG 5 (Mi-8, Mi-24); HFSA 5 (Mi-2, Mi-8, Mi-9).
- ● **Bautzen** Closed. Ex-FAG 25 (L-39ZO).
- ● **Bentlage** Immediately W of Rheine. HFR 15 (CH-53G); SSHFK 1 (Bö105M).
- ● **Berlin-Gatow** Ex-UK airhead. New base for *Luftwaffe* museum.
- ● **Berlin-Tegel** Ex-French airhead.
- ● **Berlin-Tempelhof** Ex-US airhead.
- ● **Bitburg** Reserve base from 1994. Ex-36th FW (F-15C Eagle).
- ● **Brand** Closed. Ex-116 Rgt (MiG-27).
- ● **Brandenburg** Closes 1994. Ex 2/LTS 65 (Mi-2, Mi-8).
- ● **Brandis** Closed. Ex-357 Rgt (Su-25).
- ● **Bremgarten** Closed. Ex-AG 51 (RF-4E Phantom).
- ● **Bückeburg** Immediately NE of Bückeburg. *Heeresfliegerwaffenschule* (CH-53G, UH-1D, PAH-1, Bö105M). Helicopter museum in town.

- **Celle** 3 miles (5km) SW of Celle. PAR 16 (PAH-1); HFS 1 (Alouette II); HFVS 910 (PAH-1, Bö105M, BK-117).
- **Cottbus** NW Suburbs of Cottbus. HFS 70 (Mi-8, Mi-24); Ex-KHG 3 (Mi-8), HFSA 3 (Mi-2, Mi-8, Mi-9); *Verbindungsflugkette* (An-2, Zlin 43) and HFS 400 (Bö105).
- **Damgarten** (Puttnitz) Closes 1994. Immediately E of Damgarten. 733 Rgt (MiG-29).
- **Demmin** Closed. Ex-368 Rgt (Su-25).
- **Dresden** Airport. Ex-3/LTS 65 (An-26); 439 Rgt (Mi-24); 6 Sqn (Mi-6, Mi-8).
- **Drewitz** Closed. Ex-JBFG 37 (MiG-23); TAS 87 (MiG-21RF).
- **Erding** Immediately NE of Erding. (Ground instructional aircraft only.)
- **Falkenberg** Closes 1994. 9 miles (15km) E of Torgau. 31 Rgt (MiG-29).
- **Fassberg** Immediately N of Fassberg. HFR 10 (UH-1D).
- **Finow** Closed. Ex-787 Rgt (MiG-29).
- **Finsterwalde** Closed. Ex-339 Rgt (MiG-27).
- **Fritzlar** Immediately S of Fritzlar. PAR 36 (PAH-1); HFS 2 (Alouette II).
- **Fürstenfeldbruck**. Immediately NE of Fürstenfeldbruck. JBG 49 (Alpha Jet).

- **Gross Dölln (Templin)** Closes 1994. 5½ miles (9km) SSE of Templin. 20 Rgt (Su-17).
- **Grossenhain** Closed. Ex-296 Rgt (MiG-27).
- **Gütersloh**. See army airfields.
- **Hahn** Closed. Ex-50th TFW (F-16C).
- **Hassleben** Closed. Ex-298 Rgt (Mi-2, Mi-6, Mi-8, Mi-24).
- **Husum** Closed. Ex-JBG 41 (Alpha Jet).
- **Itzehoe-Hungriger Wolf** 6 miles (3¾km) E of Hohenaspe. HFR 6 (PAH-1, UH-1D, Bö105M).
- **Juterborg** Closed. Ex-833 Rgt (MiG-23); 486 Rgt (Mi-8, Mi-24).
- **Kamenz** Closed. Ex-TFAG 45 (An-2, L.410, Zlin 43).
- **Kaufbeuren** Immediately S of Kaufbeuren. *Technischeschule* 1 (instructional airframes).
- **Kiel-Holtenau** 1 Mile (2km) N of Holtenau. MFG 5 (Sea King, Skyservant).
- **Köln-Bonn** Immediately E of Wahn. Cologne Airport. *Flugbereitschaftsstaffel* (Airbus, B707, VFW614, Challenger, UH-1D).
- **Kothen** Closed. Ex-85 Rgt (MiG-29).
- **Lahr-Hugsweier**. Closed. Ex-444 Squadron (CH-136).
- **Landsberg** (Penzing). 1¾ miles (3km) NE of Landsberg. LTG 61 (Transall C.160D, UH-1D).
- **Laupheim** 2½ miles (4km) SE of Laupheim. HFR 25 (CH-53G); SSHFK 2 (Bö105M).
- **Leck** Closed. Ex-AG 52 (RF-4E Phantom).
- **Leipheim**. (Dornier Skyservant — storage and sale)
- **Mahlwinkel** Closed. Ex-127 Rgt (Mi-6, Mi-8, Mi-24); 296 Sqn (Mi-6).
- **Manching** (Ingoldstadt) Immediately SE of Manching. *Wehrtechnischedienststelle* 61 (trials aircraft). DASA factory.
- **Mendig (Niedermendig)** 1 Mile (2km) SE of Niedermendig. HFR 35 (CH-53G); SSHFK 3 (Bö105M).
- **Merseburg** Closed. Ex-73 Rgt (MiG-29).
- **Mirow** (Laerz) Closed. Ex-19 Rgt (MiG-27).
- **Neubrandenburg** (Trollenhagen) Closed. Ex-JFG 2 (MiG-21MF); *Verbindungsflugkette* (An-2, Zlin 43).
- **Neuhardenberg** (Marxwalde). Closed. Ex-JFG 8 (MiG-21bis); LTG 65 (Tu-134, Tu-152, Il-62, Mi-8, L.410).

- **Neuhausen** Closed. Ex-HFR 20 (UH-1D); HFS 10 (Bö105M).
- **Neuruppin** Closed. Ex-730 Rgt (Su-17).
- **Niederstetten** Immediately SE of Niederstetten. HFR 30 (UH-1D); HFS 12 (Alouette II).
- **Oldenburg** Closed. Ex-JBG 43 (Alpha Jet).
- **Oranienburg** Closed. Ex-33 Rgt (Mi-6, Mi-8, Mi-17); 292 Sqn Mi-8ECM.
- **Parchim** Closed. Ex-172 Rgt (Mi-24).
- **Parow** 10 miles (6km) N of Stralsund. MHG 18 (Mi-8, Mi-14).
- **Peenemünde** Closed. Ex-JFG 9 (MiG-23); *Zieldartstellungskette* (L-39).
- **Pferdsfeld** (Sobernheim) Closes 1994. Ex-JBG 35 (F-4F Phantom).
- **Preschen** Closed. Ex-TAS 47 (MiG-21RF).
- **Rhein-Main** 7½ miles (12km) SW of Frankfurt-am-Main. Frankfurt Airport. USAF Air Mobility Command airhead.
- **Rotenburg** Closed. Ex-HFS 3 (Alouette III).
- **Roth** 1¾ miles (3km) SSE of Roth-bei-Nürnburg. PAR 26 (PAH-1).
- **Rothenburg** Closed. Ex-FAG 15 (MiG-21U).
- **Schönefeld**. Immediately S of Schönefeld. Berlin Airport. Ex-3/*Flugbereitshaftstaffel* (L.410, Mi-8).
- **Sembach** Immediately S of Sembach. HQ USAF 17th Air Force (no residents).
- **Söllingen** (Baden-Söllingen). Closed. Ex-409, 421 & 439 Sqn (CF-18 Hornet).
- **Sperenberg** 6 miles (10km) NE of Luckenwalde. Closes 1994. 226 Rgt (transport/ECM).
- **Stendal** Closed. Ex-76 & 440 Rgts (Mi-8, Mi-17, Mi-24).
- **Straubing (Mitterhartshausen)** 3¾ miles (6km) S of Straubing. HFS 4 (Bö105M).
- **Weimar-Nohra** Closed. Ex-336 Rgt (Mi-8, Mi-24).
- **Welzow** Closed. Ex-11 Rgt (Su-24).
- **Werneuchen** Closed. Ex-931 Rgt (MiG-25R); - Sqn (Mi-2, Mi-6, Mi-24).
- **Wildenrath** Closed. Ex-19 and 92 Sqn (Phantom FGR2); 60 Sqn (Andover); 12 Flight (Gazelle).
- **Wittstock** Closes 1994. 3 miles (5km) NNE of Wittstock. 33 Rgt (MiG-29).
- **Wunsdorf** 2½ miles (4km) N of Wunsdorf. LTG 62 (Transall C.160, UH-1D).
- **Zerbst** Closed. Ex-35 Rgt (MiG-29).
- **Zweibrucken** Closed. Ex-26th RW (RF-4C Phantom); 10th MAS (C-23A).

OTHER ARMY BASES:

Foreign army bases in Germany are detailed below. All are US Army unless otherwise stated. More units may have been withdrawn by the time this book is published.

- **Ansbach** 3 miles (5km) ENE of Ansbach. 2-1 Avn (AH-64A, OH-58C); 3-1 Avn (AH-64A, OH-58C); 7-1 Avn (UH-60A, EH-60A, OH-58D, UH-1H); 45 Medical Coy (UH-60A).
- **Bad Kreuznach** E of town, between Bad Kreuznach and Bosenheim. 7-227 Avn, Det (UH-1H).
- **Bad Tolz** 1¾ miles (3km) ESE of Bad Tolz. 10 SFG (UH-1H).
- **Baden** ½ mile (1km) NW of Oos. (French) 12 GHL (Alouette III).
- **Büdingen** 1-1 Cavalry (AH-1F, OH-58C).
- **Butzweilerhof** 4¼ miles (7km) NW of Köln. (Belgian) 16 Rgt (Alouette, A.109)
- **Coleman Barracks** Immediately S of Lampertheim. 6-158 Avn (CH-47); 3-7 Cav (AH-1F, OH-58A); 7 Sigs Brig (U-21A).
- **Detmold** W outskirts of Detmold. (British) Nos 654, 659 & 669 Sqn (= 4 Regiment — Lynx, Gazelle). To Wattisham 1995.
- **Feucht** 1 mile (2km) W of Feucht. 4-2 Avn (AH-1F, OH-58C, UH-60A, EH-60A).
- **Giebelstadt** Immediately ESE of Giebelstadt. 3-135 Avn (UH-60A); 7-158 Avn (OH-58D, UH-60A); 5-159 Avn (CH-47D).
- **Göppingen** Immediately E of Göppingen. 3-1 Inf (OH-58A, UH-1H).
- **Grafenwohr** Immediately SE of Grafenwohr. 7 ATC (UH-1H).
- **Gütersloh** 3 miles (5km) NW of Gütersloh. (British) Nos 651, 652 and 661 Sqn (= 1 Regiment — Lynx/Gazelle) from Hildesheim.
- **Hanau** 1¾ miles (3km) ENE of Bruchköbel. 2-227 Avn (AH-64A, OH-58C); 3-227 Avn (AH-64A, OH-58C); 7-227 Avn (UH-60A, EH-60A, UH-1H, OH-58A/D).
- **Heidelberg** Immediately SE of Schwetzingen. 207 Avn Coy (UH-1H, C-12).
- **Hildesheim** Immediately N of Hildesheim. (British) Nos 651, 652 & 661 Sqn (= 1 Regiment — Gazelle). To Gütersloh 1995.
- **Illesheim** 1 mile (2km) S of Illesheim. 2-6 Avn (AH-64A, OH-58C); 6-6 Avn (AH-64A, OH-58C); 4-229 Avn (AH-64A, OH-58C).
- **Landstuhl** S of Ramstein AFB. 236 Medical Coy (UH-60A).
- **Merzbrück** 5½ miles (9km) NE of Aachen. (Belgian) 18 Rgt (A.109).
- **Schwabisch** 2½ miles (4km) NE of Schwabisch Hall. 6-159 Avn (UH-60A).
- **Stuttgart-Echterdingen** (Airport) NW of Bernhausen. HQ USEUCOM (C-12C); 4-159 Avn (OH-58D, UH-1H).
- **Trier** Immediately SW of Trier; west bank of Moselle. (French) Esc 1 Corps (Alouette III, Gazelle).
- **Werl** Immediately N of Werl. (Belgian) 17 Rgt (A.109).
- **Wiesbaden** 5 miles (8km) SE of Wiesbaden, SE of Erbenheim. 1 MIB (RC-12K); 3-58 Avn (U-21A, UH-1H); 5-158 Avn (U-21A, C-12C, UH-1H); 159 Medical Coy (UH-60A); 7-159 Avn (UH-1H).

The last A-10A Thunderbolt IIs in Europe are based at Spangdahlem with the 52nd FW. A single squadron was transferred from the UK in January 1993. *Paul Jackson*

IRELAND

The *Aer-Chór na h'Éireann*/Irish Air Corps has a fleet of over 40 aircraft for surveillance, fisheries protection, communications/VIP, SAR and light attack. In the last-mentioned role are six armed Fouga Magisters, although weapons can also be carried by SF.260 trainers and Cessna 172 observation aircraft.

Shortly after the Republic of Ireland gained independence from the UK, the IAC was formed, gaining its initial aircraft, an Avro 504K, in July 1922. Until the first Alouette III arrived in 1963, all equipment was obtained from Great Britain. First jets were Vampire T11s delivered from 1956, although two-seat Spitfire trainers were used until 1960.

A maritime surveillance capability was obtained in 1977 with delivery of a Super King Air and is being greatly expanded during 1994 with two patrol-configured CN.235s to complement an earlier delivery of this type in transport guise. In recent years, consideration has been given to an attack helicopter and replacement of the Magisters by ex-German

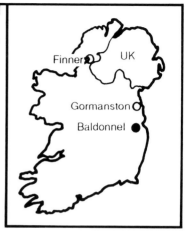

Alpha Jets. Air shows are held regularly at Baldonnel.

In view of the security situation in Ireland, lurking near any military installation is not recommended.

BALDONNEL (CASEMENT)

Location: 8 miles SW of Dublin
ICAO code: EIME
Runway: 05/23 (4,800ft/1,463m); 11/29 (6,000ft/1,829m)
Telephone: Dublin 592493

Most IAC aircraft will be found at Baldonnel. No 1 Support Wing comprises a Super King Air and Gulfstream IV of Transport & Training Squadron; six Magisters of Light Strike Squadron; and CN.235s of Maritime Squadron. Included in No 3 Support Wing are two Gazelles of the Helicopter School; seven Alouette IIIs of Army Support Squadron; five Dauphins of Naval Support Squadron; and an Alouette III of SAR Squadron. Flying instruction is also undertaken at Baldonnel with the Training Wing which has eight SF.260WEs in the Basic Flying Training School and one Magister on loan to the Advanced FTS.

Views over the airfield are restricted by geography. The eastern perimeter road by the 23 threshold is, unfortunately, below the height of the ramp and is useful only on rare occasions when runway 23 is in use. Aircraft approaching runway 29 can be photographed from the road which again, is below airfield level. No loitering is permitted when VIP aircraft are expected, In compensation, however, the IAC looks favourably upon written applications to tour the base when made by groups belonging to an aviation society.

Baldonnel is named after the patriot, Sir Roger Casement, and exhibits an intriguing mixture of infrastructure styles which range from World War 1 hangars to the characterless sheds of today. Final RAF residents were the Bristol F2bs of No 100 Sqn which departed on 4 February 1922. Thereafter the histories of Baldonnel and the IAC are inextricably linked, progressing through F2bs, DH9s, various Avro trainers, Gladiators, Hinds, Lysanders, Hectors, Ansons, Miles Magisters, Hurricanes, Masters, Seafires, Chipmunks, Provosts, Vampire T11s, Doves and BAe 125s to the aircraft of the present.

Longest-serving aircraft are the Alouettes, the first of which was received in November 1963. Service-entry dates for

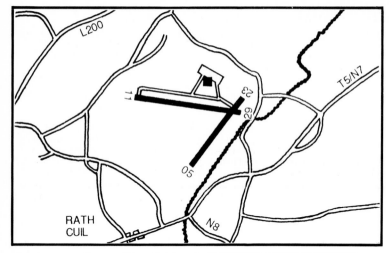

other types are: Cessna 172 — October 1972; Magister — May 1975; King Air and SF.260 — March 1977; Gazelle — December 1979; Dauphin — September 1985; Gulfstream IV — January 1990; and CN.235 — June 1991.

OTHER MILITARY AIR BASES:

- **Finner Camp** 1 mile (2km) NE of Bundoran. Detachments (one Dauphin; two Alouette III)
- **Gormanston** Immediately N of Gormanston. No 2 Support Wing/Army Co-operation Squadron (seven Reims-Cessna 172Hs).

Many of Baldonnel's buildings remain from the RAF days. The old hangar and huts behind this SF.260 contrast with the large, modern hangar in the distance. *Tony Kearns*

NETHERLANDS

Since May 1991, when the last Canadair-Northrop NF-5 was withdrawn, the *Koninklijke Luchtmacht* (KLu) has possessed an all-F-16 front line. At peak strength, nine squadrons were equipped, but this is being reduced by two during 1994-96 whilst a further two squadrons have a training role. In effect, the number of fighters declared to NATO is falling from 162 to 108. Also now gone — withdrawn between October 1993 and January 1994 — are the F-15A/B Eagles formerly based at (Soesterberg Camp New Amsterdam) with the USAF's 32nd FG.

Despite these reductions, some new equipment will be found on KLu airfields in coming years, although much of it will be assigned to the air force's *Groep Helikopters*, a component specifically assigned to army support. Presently equipped with Alouette IIIs and Bö105s, the *Gp Heli* is to receive Chinooks, Cougars and a new attack helicopter to be operated from Eindhoven and Gilze-Rijen. The current *Gp Heli* base at Deelen is to close by 1997, following the running-down of Ypenburg in 1994. With the regular RNethAF, two C-130H Hercules have

arrived since January 1994 to begin the process of replacing the venerable F.27 Friendship/Troopship and they will be followed in 1995 by two DC-10 tankers and four Fokker 50s. Two new executive jets may also be ordered. Early in 1994, three new AB 412SPs replaced the Alouettes based at Leeuwarden for SAR.

Naval aviation, the *Marine Luchtvaartdienst*, is part of the Royal Netherlands Navy, the *Koninklijke Marine*. This operates from two home bases: Valkenburg for fixed-wing and de Kooij for helicopters.

Most air bases are on sites used before or during World War 2. Ypenburg, Gilze-Rijen and Valkenburg were amongst the first to be returned to service, followed by the former *Luftwaffe* fighter base at Twente. As the result of an official revision of the Dutch language, the last-mentioned is now known as Twenthe. Gloster Meteors were the KLu's first jet fighters, going initially to Twenthe during 1948, then to the new interceptor station at Leeuwarden.

Thereafter came US-supplied F-84Gs and F-84Fs for the fighter-bomber wings at Eindhoven and Volkel. Hunters built locally by Fokker, as well as Italian-produced F-86K Sabres served in the air defence role from Soesterberg, Leeuwarden and Twenthe. The front line was rationalised to two aircraft types during the 1960s and 1970s when Starfighters were used for interception and interdiction, backed by NF-5As in the light attack role.

There is normally a KLu air base open to the public each year, but anniversaries are marked by additional events.

EINDHOVEN

Location: 3¾ miles (6km) W of Eindhoven
ICAO code: EHEH
Runway: 04/22 (9,846ft/3,001m)

Vliegbasis Eindhoven (also known as Welschap) is undergoing a change of resident squadrons and aircraft and will become the KLu's main transport base, both fixed-wing and helicopter. The F.27s of No 334 Sqn are already in residence and are being replaced by Hercules from 1994, followed by DC-10s (1995), Fokker 60s (1996) and new VVIP light jets. F-16 training squadron, No 316 Sqn disbanded on 1 April 1994 and its facilities will be used during exercises by the recce-tasked F-16A(R)s of No 306 Sqn from Volkel. The F-16s previously resident carried the *Were Di* fin stripe of a white band with black wolves' heads which is also worn at Gilze-Rijen. For the future, No 298 Sqn will move-in from Soesterberg and exchange its Alouettes for 17 AS 532U2 Cougars from January 1996 onwards and No 300 Sqn will transfer from Deelen to gain six new and seven ex-Canadian CH-47 Chinooks.

Both approaches are close to public roads and a good view of flying can be obtained from the civil terminal.

The new NATO base at Eindhoven opened on 1 May 1952, on which day the seal was set on its future use as a fighter-bomber base by formation of No 314 Sqn with F-84G Thunderjets. Two more similarly-equipped squadrons were raised on 1 July 1952 (No 315) and 1 April 1953 (No 316, staffed by reservists). No 316 disbanded in May 1955 to be reborn as a regular unit with F-84F Thunderstreaks on 1 August 1956. Its companions were likewise re-equipped by April 1957, although No 316 disbanded in January 1958 to keep the other two squadrons up to strength. No 315 moved to Twenthe in May 1970, leaving No 314 to be the final KLu operator of the F-84F, the last of which was relinquished on 21 December 1970.

The NF-5 era at Eindhoven began with first deliveries in November 1969, allowing No 314 Sqn to be declared operational on 1 March 1972. No 316 re-formed with NF-5s on 1 July 1971, transferring to Gilze (26 April 1972) before becoming operational. In a further swap in preparation for F-16As, No 316 was installed at Eindhoven in May 1988 and No 314 proceeded to Gilze the following September. Having been slated for closure because of noise complaints, Eindhoven underwent a profound change of fortunes when a major rebuilding programme gave it a new runway (04/22) opened on 2 July 1984. No 316 stood-down with the KLu's last NF-5s on 1 May 1991 and immediately began training on F-16s. The squadron officially re-formed on 1 October 1991

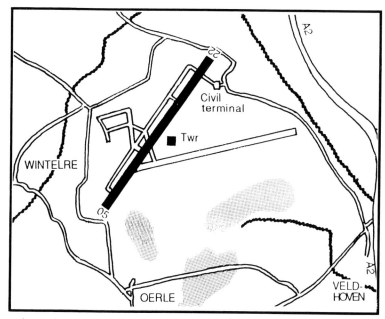

and served as a non-operational conversion unit until disbanded on 1 April 1994. No 334's F.27s arrived from Soesterberg on 18 May 1992 and began phasing-out when the first aircraft was put into storage at Eindhoven on October 1993. The first KLu Hercules was handed-over in the USA on 24 January 1994 and then went to Belgium for crew training.

LEEUWARDEN

Location: Immediately NW of Leeuwarden
ICAO code: EHLW
Runway: 06/24 (9,675ft/2,949m); 09/27 (6,613ft/2,016m)

Sole military air base in the north of the Netherlands, Leeuwarden has two F-16A Fighting Falcon squadrons. No 322 (parrot badge) is assigned to NATO's rapid reaction force and No 323 (an Amazon archer) has been the Tactical Training Evaluation & Standards Squadron since 3 July 1992. The KLu's rescue flight, the *SAR Vlucht* is replacing its Alouette IIIs by Agusta-Bell 412SPs during 1994. All resident aircraft wear the Friesland colours of a red kidney-shaped motif on a blue and white striped background.

Runway 06/24 is used for normal operations. Aircraft landing on 24 can be photographed from the road at Jelsum, but the taxyway is distant. At the 06 end there is a better view of taxying aircraft from a blocked road near the threshold. The base receives several visitors in connection with the North Sea air combat range.

No 1 Sqn flew into Leeuwarden from Twente with its Meteor F4s on 28 January 1949, becoming No 323 Sqn on 14 April 1949 before retreating whence it came on 1 May 1950. The Meteor presence was maintained, however, with formation of No 324 on 1 May 1949, No 325 on 15 November 1949 and No 326 on 2 October 1950. After converting to F8s, the Leeuwarden Meteor wing lost No 326 to Twenthe in April 1952, in exchange for the F4s of No 323, which were not replaced by F8s until 1954. On 28 December 1955, No 325 received the KLu's first Hunter F4. No 324 began Hunter conversion in April 1956, although No 323 did not fly its first Hunter mission until 18 October 1957. The latter was an OCU until 1960 and operated several Hunter T7s alongside the F4s. In October

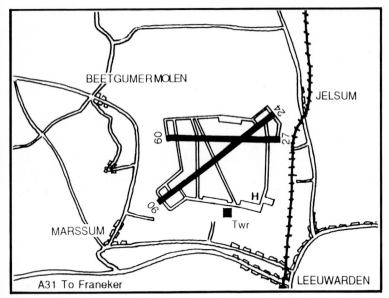

1957, 324 Squadron upgraded to Hunter F6s and apart from a few months at Twenthe remained such until disbanded at Leeuwarden on 1 April 1964. No 325 went to Soesterberg, still with F4s, in March 1958.

The present partnership at Leeuwarden was established when No 322 Sqn formed on 1 April 1964 with pilots trained on Starfighters by No 306. Meanwhile No 323 had stood-down with Hunters on 1 September 1963 and retrained as an F-104 squadron which became operational on 1 October 1965. The interceptor role previously held by the Leeuwarden wing was diluted with a 60% attack tasking after conversion to F-16s. Both squadrons were put under a single CO on 16 April 1979 and unofficially known as '645 Squadron' (the sum of the two numbers).

Delivery of F-16s to Leeuwarden for training began on 7 June 1979 and an OCU, the TCA, was established on 1 October the same year. On completion of training by the TCA, No 322 became operational with Fighting Falcons on 1 May 1981. After withdrawing its last F-104 on 1 April 1980, No 323 was similarly declared on 1 April 1982 as the KLu's second F-16 squadron. TCA disbanded on 1 March 1986. The SAR Flight and its

Alouette IIIs moved-in from Soesterberg on 1 July 1977. Hand-over of the first *KLu* Agusta-Bell 214SP took place on 21 December 1993, the Alouette phase-out beginning eight days earlier with departure of H-20 to the museum at Soesterberg.

TWENTHE
Location: 3¾ miles (6km) ENE of Hengelo
ICAO code: EHTW
Runway: 06/24 (9,801ft/2,987m); 11/29 (6,558ft/1,999m)

Two squadrons of F-16 Fighting Falcons are based at *Vliegbasis* Twenthe, jointly tasked with air defence and attack. Both wear the *Twents Ros* red fin band with white rampant horses and are individually No 313 Sqn (tiger's head badge) and No 315 Sqn (lion's head). No 315 is assigned to the NATO rapid reaction force and No 313 took-over the OCU role on 1 April 1994 from No 316 at Eindhoven. It is planned to disband No 315 Sqn in 1996.

The main runway (06/24) is accessible at both ends from blocked roads. At the 06 end the required road is a sand track by the Kokpit restaurant.

No less than 16 RAF and Allied squadrons passed through Airfield B106 between April and September 1945, including the Dutch No 322 which re-formed here with Spitfire IXs on 27 September 1946. Following a period of service in the East Indies it moved to Soesterberg in August 1951. Naval aviation was represented by No 320 Sqn which arrived from the UK with Mitchells, but disbanded on 1 May 1946. Meanwhile, the *Jagdvlieg School* (JVS) had formed on 19 July 1946 with Spitfires and Oxfords as the fighter pilots' school. The RNethAF's first jets — Meteor F4s — began arriving at the JVS on 27 June 1948, leading to formation of No 1 Sqn at Twenthe on 15 November that year. Departing to Leeuwarden in January 1949, the squadron returned with its new number, No 323, in May 1950 and remained until April 1952. The same month, No 326 and its Meteor F8s were posted-in and stayed until December 1956. Its new base was Woensdrecht, to where the JVS had moved the previous June.

For the next seven years, Twenthe was an all-weather fighter base equipped with F-86K Sabres. No 701 Sqn formed on 1 June 1956, followed by No 702 five months later, the latter in the training role from November 1960 until disbanded in April 1962. During the Sabre era, No 324's Hunter F6s were briefly resident between September 1958 and July 1959. No 701 disappeared on 1 July 1963, by which time the base was hosting the KLu's first Starfighters. No 306 Sqn began working-up in May 1963 before adopting RF-104Gs later in the year for the recce role. An OCU, 'The Dutch Masters' started receiving TF-104Gs in June 1963 and remained at Twenthe until disbanded on 1 January 1969, whilst No 306 moved to Volkel on 3 September the same year.

The Starfighter's somewhat retrograde replacement at Twenthe was the venerable Lockheed T-33A. The *Transitie Vliegopleiding* arrived from Woensdrecht on 14 October 1968 and eventually flew its last T-33 mission on 9 June 1972. In December 1969, the base began another lease of life with delivery of the first factory-fresh NF-5s. No 315 Sqn was established with the aircraft on 1 May 1970 and the TVO was reborn as No 313 Sqn on 12 October 1972 as the OCU. An F-16

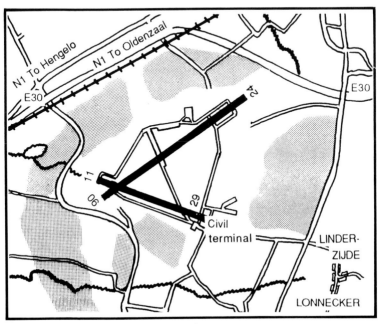

temporary conversion unit was installed at Twenthe on 1 March 1986 as a result of which No 315 became operational with Fighting Falcons on 1 November 1987 and No 313 disbanded as an NF-5 squadron on 1 July 1988 before rejoining the front line with F-16s on 1 April 1990 — the last unit so to do.

VALKENBURG

Location: 2½ miles (4km) SE of Katwijk.
ICAO code: EHVB
Runway: 05/23 (8,044ft/2,452m); 17/35 (4,920ft/1,500m)

Long-range maritime patrol is undertaken from *Marinevliegkamp* Valkenburg by Nos 320 and 321 Sqn, flying a pool of 13 Lockheed P-3C Orions. No 321 also functions as the OCU following disbandment of No 2 Sqn on 1 June 1991. Foreign maritime aircraft are often seen at the base.

The main ramp is on the west side of the airfield. Normally, only the 05/23 runway is used and both thresholds are served by minor roads which provide good vantage points. A road from Valkenburg village to the 17 threshold gives views of aircraft taxying on the north side of the secondary runway.

Built in 1939, Valkenburg became home to No 6 Sqn's Austers in 1945, but the unit moved-out in June 1946 to be replaced by 1 *Transportvlieg Afdeling* with a variety of transport types. Becoming No 334 Sqn on 1 December 1952, this moved to Ypenburg in December 1957. Meanwhile, in February 1946, No 861 Sqn transferred the first Fairy Fireflies from the UK to Valkenburg, where they were also used by the *Gevechtsvliegopleiding*, or fighter pilot's school. The station was commissioned as a naval base on 15 October 1947 and since then has been synonymous with naval aviation, having seen almost every squadron either form there or pass through.

Residents have included Nos 1, 2, 3, 4, 5, 7, 8, 320, 321, 860 and 861 Sqn. Aircraft types have progressed through the Sea Fury, Harpoon, SH-34J Seabat, Avenger, Sea Hawk, Tracker and AB 204B. In more recent times, No 320 Sqn's first four Orions were delivered to Valkenburg on 21 July 1982 after training in the USA and No 321 flew its final SP-13A Atlantic sortie on 28 December 1984.

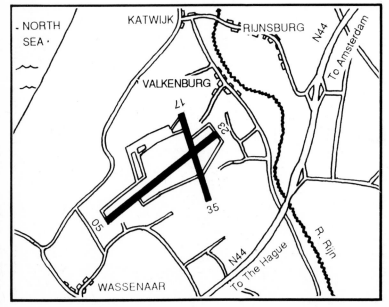

VOLKEL

Location: 1¾ miles (3km) ENE of Volkel
ICAO code: EHVK
Runway: 06L/24R (9,920ft/3,024m);
06R/24L 9,329ft/2,843m)

Two F-16A fighter-bomber/air defence squadrons are stationed at Volkel, together with F-16A(R)s of recce-tasked No 306. The last-mentioned has an eagle's head badge; No 311 Sqn uses an eagle landing; and No 312 has two swords crossed upon a flash of lightning. The base is also home to the *Testgroep KLu* which has a single F-16 marked with the KLu badge of a crown and an eagle upon a miniature of the national roundel. All residents wear the regional markings of Noord Brabant in the form of a red/white checked fin stripe. No 306 deploys to its war base at Eindhoven during exercises, having used de Peel until early 1994.

Aircraft operate from shelters north of the runways. Both approaches and the northeast taxyway can be photographed from roads or tracks at each end of the main runway.

Following rebuilding, the ex-*Luftwaffe* base at Volkel was originally designated an interceptor station. No 327 Sqn formed with Meteor F4s on 1 December 1950, followed by No 328 on 15 May 1951. However, No 327 moved-out in the same

month and its companion was posted in October. The change occurred as the result of Volkel being transferred to the tactical air force on 3 April 1951 for use by a fighter-bomber wing. A month later, on 1 May, No 311 Sqn formed with Thunderjets — the first in the Netherlands — and was joined by No 312 on 1 December that year. On 1 December 1952, the T-33As which had entered service with the Base Flight in August 1952 formed a fighter school, the *Jachtvliegschool* II, and this added F-84Gs 12 months later to become No 313 Sqn.

The KLu accepted its initial F-84F Thunderstreaks at Volkel on 9 December 1955 and equipped No 311 first, with Nos 312 and 313 following by the end of 1956. On 1 July 1960, No 311 became the Netherlands' first tactical nuclear squadron using US-supplied warheads. No 313 had moved to Woensdrecht in June 1958 and its place was belatedly, yet briefly, taken when No 306 and its RF-84Fs moved-in from Deelen in December 1962, staying only until May 1963. Volkel's last F-84Fs were withdrawn from No 312 Sqn on 1 December 1965.

Volkel was the final base to receive Starfighters. No 311 Sqn was declared operational on the F-104G on 3 March 1965, followed by No 312 on 9 March 1966, and the strike/attack wing was

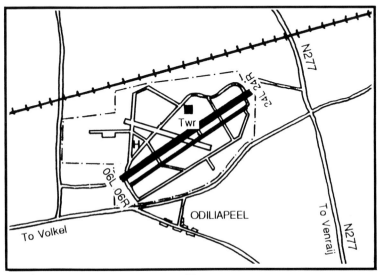

strengthened when No 306's RF-104Gs were added on 3 September 1969. Conversion to the current F-16 began when the first aircraft was delivered for No 311 Sqn on 1 June 1982 and the unit became operational on 1 July 1984. No 306 followed with its F-16A(R) recce aircraft on 1 October 1984 and 12 months after that it was the turn of No 312. The last-mentioned had stood-down on 14 June 1984 and passed the KLu's final Starfighters to a holding unit at Volkel, from where a formation farewell mission was flown on 21 November 1985. US nuclear weapons were withdrawn from No 311 Sqn in 1989 and Volkel has provided F-16s for QRA interception since 8 January 1993.

OTHER MILITARY AIR BASES:

● **Deelen** 5½ miles (9km) NNW of Arnhem. No 299 Sqn (Bö105C); No 300 Sqn (Alouette III); No 302 Sqn (Alouette III). Airfield closes in 1997. Technical school at Groot Heidekamp, Schaarsbergen, south of airfield (instructional airframes).
● **Gilze-Rijen** 1 mile (2km) N of Gilze. No 314 Sqn (F-16A). KLu depot (aircraft overhaul and storage)
● **de Kooij** Immediately SE of den Helder. Nos 7 and 860 Sqn (SH-14D Lynx).
● **de Peel** 5 miles (8km) W of Venraij. Reserve base.
● **Soesterberg** Immediately N of Soesterberg village. No 298 Sqn (Alouette III). To close. KLu Museum at Kamp Zeist, S of E30 motorway.
● **Woensdrecht** Closed.
● **Ypenburg** 5 miles (8km) SSE of Bergen op Zoom. Reserve base and Fokker plant. *Elementaire Militaire Vliegopleiding* (Pilatus PC-7).

Orions of the Netherlands Navy are based at Valkenburg, although one is permanently detached to Iceland. *Paul Jackson*

Most famous of the RNethAF's fighter squadrons is No 322 at Leeuwarden. *Paul Jackson*

PORTUGAL

Long overdue modernisation of the *Força Aérea Portuguesa* (FAP) was achieved in mid-1994 with delivery of the first effective interceptors to be acquired in over 30 years. Lockheed F-16 Fighting Falcons supplant A-7P Corsairs and armed T-38A Talon jet trainers which have hitherto provided the air defence of this NATO founder-member. Combat effectiveness has also been boosted by the supply of ex-German Alpha Jets for light attack duties, replacing Fiat G.91Rs, the last of which were withdrawn in June 1993. Additionally promised by the US are 52 second-hand UH-1H Iroquois helicopters and 10 AH-1F Cobras for the planned army aviation force at Tancos, whilst the newly-formed naval air arm has recently obtained five Westland Lynx for operation from its frigates.

Untouched by World War 2, Portuguese air bases have developed without interruption since their foundation. The secondary airfield at Aveiro/Sao Jacinto was opened in April 1918 to train French naval pilots and Tancos, handed over to the army in 1993, was inaugurated in 1924. Not all FAP facilities have such a long pedigree, however. NATO-inspired expansion resulted in the opening of Monte Real in 1959, whilst Beja was built with German money and became operational in the second half of 1966 as a *Luftwaffe* training base. Its Alpha Jets were withdrawn at the end of 1993 and the facilities turned over to Portugal.

Membership of NATO brought the FAP jet aircraft such as F-84G Thunderjets and F-86 Sabres during the 1950s, but much of the armed forces' efforts were directed against liberation movements in the African possessions during the following decade. German-supplied G.91Rs were also employed abroad until a coup of 1974 ended overseas intervention but severely restricted investment in the FAP. Rebuilding began with further G.91 deliveries and purchase from the US of A-7P Corsairs during the early 1980s.

The present system of squadron (*esquadra*) and wing (*grupo*) numbers was initiated in February 1978. Prior to this, units were known by their function and

base, for example *Esq de Ataque BA-5* would have been the ground attack squadron stationed at *Base Aérea* 5, Monte Real.

Military air shows are infrequent, but not unknown in Portugal. The last major event was at Ovar in 1993.

BEJA

Location: 5½ miles (9km) NW of Beja
ICAO code: LPBJ
Runways: 01L/19R (11,319ft/3,450m);
01R/19L (9,682ft/2,951m)

Base Aerea 11 greatly increased its importance to the FAP during 1993 with the installation of new flying units. *Esquadra* 103 and 301 are both equipped with Alpha Jets, operating in the advanced training and ground attack roles, respectively. Epsilon piston-emgined lightplanes of *Esq* 101 provide the primary stage of Portuguese military flying training, whilst the Alouette IIIs of *Esq* 552 are used for observation, SAR, medical evacuation and similar general duties. Activities at the base are controlled by *Grupo Operacional* 111.

Not to be confused with the small civil airfield 3 miles (5km) north of Beja, the military base is in remote terrain with no convenient public roads from which to view activities. To the east are the River Odearce and Beja-Cuba railway line.

Seeking a training and exercise base with a weather record better than the average in west-central Europe, West Germany funded construction of the base at Beja and began moving-in during the second half of 1966. In addition to a pair of UH-1D helicopters for SAR, the airfield hosted detachments of combat and transport aircraft and eventually gained its own light attack training unit. *Luftwaffen Ubungsplatzkommando Beja* formed on 29 May 1980 and received 18 Alpha Jets which, in wartime would have transferred to Leipheim as JBG 44. Activities were concluded in December 1993, by which time the 18 Alphas had passed to Portuguese control.

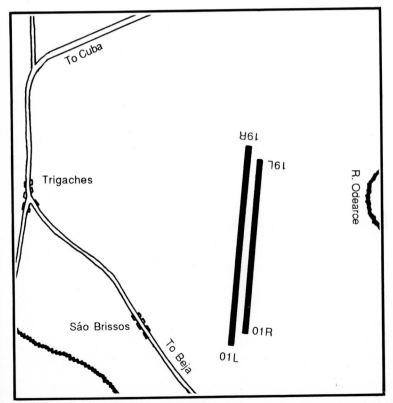

Early in 1987, the Lockheed T-33As and Northrop T-38As of *Esq* 103 were detached from *Grupo* 51 Monte Real to conduct their training in the less congested airspace around Beja. The T-33s were withdrawn in September 1991 and the T-38s on 29 June 1993, immediately following which the instructors of 103 Squadron began Alpha Jet conversion in Germany. They were joined by the staff of *Esq* 301, who had left their retired G.91s at Montijo and transferred to Beja on 1 July 1993. Delivery of 50 Alphas from Germany began on 21 September with the first five, the total comprising 18 already based at Beja and 32 from Germany, although five will be broken-down for spare parts. *Esq* 101 and its Epsilons moved into Beja from Sintra on 15 June 1993, followed by *Esq* 552 and its Alouette IIIs from Tancos on 18 November. During the same month, *Grupo Operacional* 111 was established as the base controlling authority, formalizing the transfer from German to local command.

MONTE REAL

Location: 1 mile (2km) SW of Monte Real
ICAO code: LPMR
Runways: 01/19 (8,064ft/2,458m); 14/32 (3,937ft/1,200m)

During 1993, *Base Aérea* 5 was undergoing considerable enlargement and upgrading in preparation for the arrival of 17 F-16As and three F-16Bs during the second half of 1994. The aircraft are expected to form *Esquadra* 201, which will become part of *Grupo* 61, the wing controlling activities at the base. Two squadrons, Nos 302 and 304, share a pooled fleet of Vought A-7P Corsairs, whilst the base flight has a Cessna 337 for firing range observation and an SAR Alouette III.

Prior to the start of expansion works, the N349-1 road provided best views of the airfield. From a point north of the main gate it was possible to walk through scrubland to the perimeter fence. New shelters have since been built in woods on the west side to accommodate the Corsairs. F-16s will use the facilities formerly occupied by *Esc* 302.

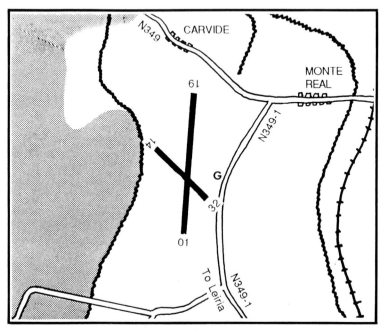

Monte Real opened on 4 October 1959 as the home of *Grupo Operacional* 501 and its two squadrons (Nos 51 and 52) of Sabres, these later forming the *Esq de Caça BA5* and then (from 1978) *Esq 201*. The veteran F-86Fs were withdrawn in August 1980, three years after arrival of T-38A advanced trainers which doubled as interceptors until passed to No 103 Sqn. The latter, although part of 51 Wing, was detached to Beja in early 1987. Its T-33As were withdrawn in September 1991 and the T-38As on 29 June 1993. Portugal's first Corsair was handed over in the USA on 18 August 1981 before delivery to newly-formed *Esq 302* at Monte Real. A follow-on batch, supplied from October 1984, permitted a second squadron to be established and declared operational late in 1985.

MONTIJO

Location: 2½ miles (4km) W of Montijo
ICAO code: LPMT
Runways: 08/26 (8,006ft/2,440m); 01/19 (7,044ft/2,147m)

Transport, maritime patrol and SAR are

the main roles of *Base Aérea* 6 following recent disbandment of the last G.91 Squadron. *Esq 501* is the FAP's C-130H Hercules unit with six aircraft; *Esq 601* operates six P-3P Orions; and *Esq 751* is equipped with five Pumas. All are under *Grupo 61*. The base strengthened its maritime connections with formation of a naval squadron (*Esquadrilha de Helicopteros de Marinha*) to fly five Lynx, the first pair of which were delivered from the UK on 24 September 1993. Montijo has facilities for NATO reinforcement aircraft in wartime.

Surrounded on three sides by water, Montijo presents major problems for the aviation enthusiast. Views from the land are distant, although a ferry service from Lisbon passes south of the base. The main ramp is north of the 08/26 runway, whilst to the south is a taxiway and numerous dispersals. The former G.91 ramp is west of the 01 threshold.

Built in 1941, Montijo was the central naval aviation base until incorporated into the FAP on its formation on 27 May 1952. The *Esquadra de Reconhecimento Maritimo* and its PV-2 Harpoons passed to the FAP as *Esq 61* and later re-equipped

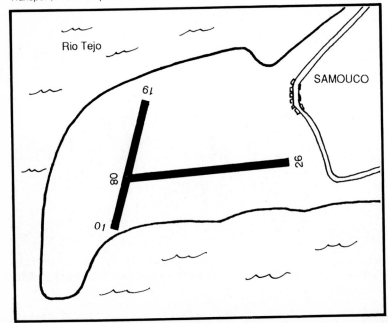

with P2V Neptunes. These were the sole FAP aircraft committed to NATO during the 1960s and when they were withdrawn in 1977, surface surveillance was undertaken by the ill-equipped Hercules. Ex-Australian P-3Bs were acquired eventually as replacements, the first emerging from modification to P-3P in July 1988.

The 16 G.91R/4s returned from the colonial wars in 1974 were installed at Montijo as *Esq* 301, but formed *Esq* 303 in January 1981 when a fresh supply of G.91R/3s was received from Germany. *Esq* 303 transferred to Lajes, Azores, where it disbanded in March 1989 and *Esq* 301 flew its final G.91 mission on 17 June 1993. First Hercules were received in 1977 to replace DC-6s, Boeing 707s and Noratlases.

OTHER MILITARY AIR BASES:

- **Aveiro/Sao Jacinto** 5 miles (8km) WNW of Aveiro. *Aerodrómo de Manobra* 2. Reserve base.
- **Lisbon International** Immediately NE of Lisbon. *Aerodrómo de Transito 1.* *Esq* 504 (Falcon 20, Falcon 50).
- **Ota** 3¾ miles (6km) NE of Alenquer. *Base Aérea* 2. *Centro de Formaçao Militar e Tecnica de Forca Aérea* (instructional airframes).
- **Ovar/Cortegaca** 4¼ miles (7km) NNW of Ovar. *Aerodrómo de Manobra* 1. Reserve base.
- **Sintra** 3 miles (5km) NE of Sintra. *Base Aérea* 1. *Grupo* 12: *Esq* 401 (C.212B Aviocar); *Esq* 502 (Aviocar); *Esq* 701 to be renumbered 505 (Cessna 337). *Academia da Força Aérea: Esq* 802 (sailplanes — RF-10, ASK-21). Storage site for air museum.
- **Tancos** 3¾ miles (6km) ENE of Tancos. Transferred to army.

Additionally BA-4 at **Lajes**, Azores (C.212, Puma and detachments of Corsairs); **Porto Santo**, Madeira — reserve base; and **Alverca** civil airfield (OGMA overhaul facility and air museum).

Portugal's main combat base is at Monte Real, the home of two A-7P Corsair squadrons sharing a pool of unmarked aircraft. This two-seat TA-7P is fitted with an AN/ALQ-131(V) jamming pod under the starboard wing. *Paul Jackson*

SPAIN

A member of NATO since May 1982, Spain retains national control over its air force and does not participate in multi-national commands. Nevertheless, membership of the Alliance has allowed the *Ejercito del Aire* (EdA) access to high technology, as indicated by its two wings of McDonnell Douglas EF-18 Hornets and participation in the Eurofighter programme. This represents no mean achievement for an air force which, only three decades previously, was flying re-engined versions of German aircraft designed in the 1930s.

Basic EdA administrative unit is the wing (*ala*) or group (*grupo*), one or more of which occupies an air base. Each component squadron (*escuadrón*) is now numbered as a function of the wing (eg, Nos 141 and 142 Sqn of 14 Wing), but this was not the case prior to 1971. Indeed, recent EdA history is regularly punctuated by renumberings and reorganisations, the latest on 1 July 1991. The last-mentioned had no effect at wing level, but abolished Combat, Tactical and Transport Commands and regrouped units of differing roles on a geographical basis, as was already the case with Canaries Command. The three new organisations are Central, Eastern and Straits (of Gibraltar) Commands, whilst there is no change to Personnel (training) Command or the miscellaneous units reporting directly to the general staff. Most aircraft carry wing badges, but prominent codes are more visible means of establishing ownership.

Spanish aerodromes have, for the most part, developed from early bases, including those used in the civil war. The country spent the World War 2 years recovering from its own conflict and was not invited to join the Western Union or NATO. Not until the signing of a bilateral defence treaty with the USA in 1953 was Spain allowed access to jet aircraft and other forms of military aid in return for

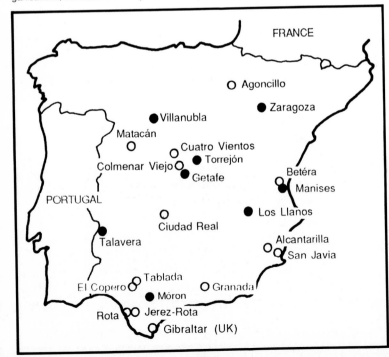

basing rights. Zaragoza and Morón were vastly expanded and new bases built at Torrejón and Rota — the last-mentioned for the US Navy — all of which are joint-user.

Initially, the USAF's Spanish airfields were required for rotations by SAC's bombers and their fighter escorts; Morón, for example went straight from grass airfield to nuclear bomber base. Later, some tactical fighter units were installed. Tanker detachments have been constant and played a key role in the 1990-91 Kuwait crisis and the 1992 aid airlift to Somalia. After some local reluctance was overcome, B-52s bombed Iraq from Morón during the Gulf War.

Following the F-86F Sabres and ground radars which gave the EdA a modern air defence network in the late 1950s, the US supplied one squadron of F-104G Starfighters and a wing of F-4C Phantoms. The locally-designed Saeta was used for ground attack and training

before being supplanted by licence-built Northrop F/RF-5As. France delivered both Mirage IIIs and Mirage F1s, whilst naval aviation, the *Arme Aérea de la Armada* became an effective attacking force on receipt of AV-8A(S) Harriers in 1976. These have now been augmented on a modern aircraft carrier by the AV-8B Harrier II version, AEW versions of Sea King and anti-submarine SH-60B Seahawks. FAMET (*Fuerzas Aeromóviles del Ejército de Tierra* — army aviation) has similarly expanded to a large force of helicopters, including Bö105s for attack and recon-naissance and a transport fleet of Iro-quois, Cougars and Chinooks. This growth has benefited the service in that its bases include two new, modern air-fields at Betera and Ciudad Real.

Military (and, for that matter, civil) air displays are a rarity in Spain, the last of note having been the Torrejón *Puertas Abiertas* ('Open Doors') in 1992 and a small event at Manises in 1993.

ALBACETE/LOS LLANOS
Location: 3 miles (5km) S of Albacete
ICAO code: LEAB
Runway: 09/27 (8,858ft/2,700m)
In 1992, Spain's entire fleet of Mirage F1s

was pooled, with Albacete's resident *Ala* 14 as the operating authority. The wing's F1CE interceptors theoretically have been joined by the multi-role F1EEs of *Ala* 46 in the Canary Islands, all now wearing '14-'

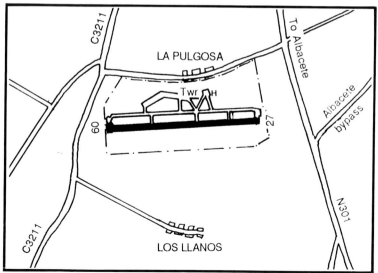

codes. In fact, *Ala* 14 now detaches numbers of both variants to the Canaries and to Manises (which see) as required.

Formerly a transport base, Albacete was home to *Grupo* 37 and two squadrons (Nos 370 and 371) of Douglas C-47s when Spain's first Caribous were delivered in January 1968 for the newly-established *Esc* 372. The Group then moved to Villanubla in order that Albacete could be upgraded for a Mirage wing. *Ala* 14 was established on 1 June 1974 and received its first aircraft on 28 June 1985 for No 141 Sqn. A follow-on order provided sufficient F1CEs for No 142 Sqn to be formed on 1 April 1980 and the position remains thus today, although there are no individual squadron markings applied to Mirages.

GETAFE
Location: Immediately S of Getafe
ICAO code: LEGT
Runway: 05/23 (8,760ft/2,670m)
This is a joint-user air base with the CASA construction and overhaul plant on the northeast side and the EdA facility to the northwest. Two wings are resident, of which *Ala* 35 (Nos 351 and 352 Sqn) is a transport unit equipped with CN.235s. *Grupo* 42 provides refresher flying for officers at desk jobs in Madrid and elsewhere, its elements being No 421 Sqn with Beech Bonanzas, No 422 Sqn with

Piper Navajos and No 423 Sqn using a mixture of Piper Aztecs and Beech Barons. An autonomous flight, *Escuadrilla* 408, is equipped with three C.212DE Aviocars specially outfitted for ELINT missions. Retired Mirage IIIEEs were collected at Getafe in 1993.

A high concrete fence along the northern perimeter road and vigilant security guards complicate ground-level viewing at Getafe. However, the footbridge of the local railway station (marked, immediately north of the 23 threshold) is an ideal vantage point for those armed with a telescope and provides views of CASA and EdA ramps as well as the approach.

This long-established airfield has been the home of CASA since its foundation in March 1923. In more recent times, 35 Wing operated the EdA's only CASA 207 Azors (No 351 Sqn until 1986), Caribous (No 353 Sqn until October 1985) and Douglas C-54s, whilst *Ala* 91 was a transport and refresher wing with C-47s, C-54s, Convair 440s, T-6 Texans, AISA I.115s, Aztecs and Navajos. Spain's first HU-16 Albatross amphibians were delivered to *Esc* 803 at Getafe on 5 December 1963 before the unit moved to Cuatro Vientos. More recently, CN.235 deliveries to 35 Wing began in December 1988 with two VIP aircraft (local designation T.19C). The regular transport T.19B was supplied from October 1990, allowing the Aviocars to re-equip 37 Wing at Villanubla.

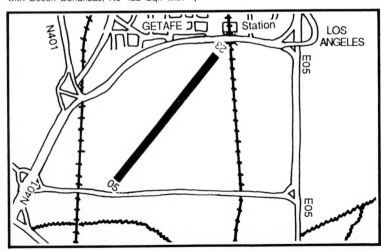

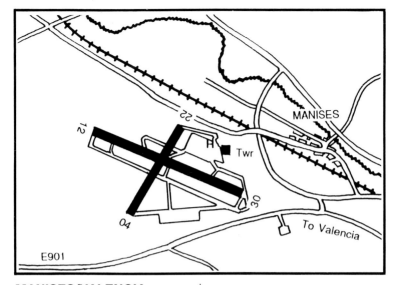

MANISES/VALENCIA

Location: 6 miles (10km) WNW of
Valencia
ICAO code: LEVC
Runways: 12/30 (8,858ft/2,700m); 04/22
(5,495ft/1,675m)

Resident military unit at this joint-user airport is — or was — *Ala de Caza* 11. Following withdrawal of Spain's Mirage IIIEE
fleet on 1 October 1992, *Ala* 11 has been
assigned a dozen Mirage F1s from the *Ala*
14 pool at Albacete-Los Llanos. The aircraft, which are normally, but not exclu-
sively F1CEs, wear 14 Wing codes.

Manises became a jet base when *Ala
de Caza* 1 formed on 6 September 1955
with two squadrons (Nos 11 and 12) of
F-86 Sabres. The redesignations of 1965
resulted in the new *Ala* 11 having *Esc* 101
for ground attack and *Esc* 112 in the air
defence role, but the squadrons were
changed again to become Nos 111 and
101, respectively, before No 111 disbanded in February 1969.

Spain acquired 24 Mirage IIIEEs and
six IIIDE trainers as replacements for the
Manises wing, the first arriving at the base
on 13 June 1970 for No 101 Sqn. No
sooner had *Esc* 103 formed than the position altered yet again in May 1971 when
the operating squadrons became Nos 111
and 112. They remained thus until No 112
disbanded on the final day of 1989 in

order to free aircraft for a proposed
Mirage upgrade. This was cancelled for
cost reasons shortly before work was due
to begin at Getafe and all the Mirage IIIs
were placed in storage for possible overseas sale.

MORON DE LA FRONTERA

Location: 9¼ miles (15km) WSW of
Morón
ICAO code: LEMO
Runway: 03/21 (11,800ft/3,597m)

Shared by the EdA and USAF, Morón is
home base to *Ala* 21 and its 18 CASA
C.101 Aviojet trainers, divided between
Esc 211 and 212. Transfer from Jerez is
planned of *Ala* 22's maritime patrol fleet
of P-3 Orions and D.3 Aviocars and half
the force was at least detached to the
base by 1993. The base is a reserve station for Air Combat Command and infrequently (usually in the autumn) hosts
training deployments of B-52s (and, from
1993, B-1s) and supporting KC-135
tankers.

As at Getafe, Spanish Railways come
to the assistance of the enthusiast with a
footbridge at Trinidad station for an elevated view of the base.

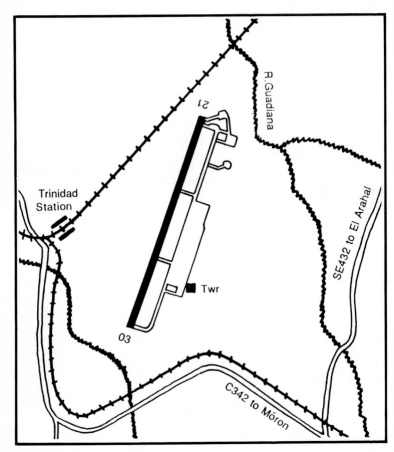

Opened in June 1941, the base was reconstructed for the USAF's SAC between September 1953 and April 1957, following which it became the 3973rd Strategic Wing and hosted B-47 Stratojet 'Reflex' deployments until March 1965. The Berlin Crisis of November 1961 brought a short-notice detachment of 157th FIS F-104C Starfighters, whilst in April 1963 Morón saw the first TAC F-105 Thunderchief deployment to Europe when the 334th TFS arrived from Seymour Johnson AFB for 90 days. Transferred from SAC to USAFE on 15 April 1966, the USAF facility became 7473rd Combat Support Group and the HC-130 Hercules of 67th ARRS moved out to Woodbridge, UK, in January 1970. The 7473rd was then inactivated and Morón placed on stand-by status, administered by Det 2 of 401st TFW.

Meanwhile, *Ala* 27 had been installed in 1956 with Hispano 2.111s (Heinkel 111s) which it flew for the film *Battle of Britain* before disbanding in the late 1960s. A more potent unit, *Ala* 5 formed with the Sabres of *Esc* 51 in May 1959 and became *Ala* 15 on 1 April 1965. On 7 January 1970, the first CASA-built Northrop SF-5 was delivered to Morón to re-equip *Esc* 202 and form *Esc* 204 nine months later.

These units became Nos 211 and 212 Sqn of *Ala* 21 in 1971, but No 212 Sqn was transferred in March 1976 on formation of No 214 with indigenous Hispano

Super Saetas. By 1980 the squadron had a strength of no less than 72 Saetas of various types, all of them withdrawn on the last day of 1981 in anticipation of the arrival of *Esc* 212. F-5s of 21 Wing twice saw action, although in both cases they were detached to the Canary Islands in 1974 and 1975 to fly a total of some 500 sorties over the disputed Spanish Sahara. In the wake of plans to concentrate the F-5 force at Talavera, *Ala* 21's aircraft were either transferred or placed in storage at Morón. Replacement Aviojets arrived early in 1993.

TALAVERA LA REAL-BADAJOZ

Location: 7½ miles (12km) E of Badajoz
ICAO code: LEBZ
Runway: 13/31 (9,350ft/2,850m)
Spain's remaining licence-built Northrop SF-5s are now based at Talavera with *Ala* 23 and its two squadrons, *Esc* 231 and 232. The original two-seat F-5Bs of this Air Combat School (*Escuela de Combate Aéreo*) were augmented in 1993 by a small number of SF-5As and SRF-5As withdrawn from *Ala* 21 at Morón. At the time, several SF-5Bs were with CASA for

rework. The Dornier 27s previously with No 231 Sqn adopted '40-' codes in 1993, indicating formation of *Grupo* 40.

The *Escuela de Reactores* (Jet School) formed at Talavera in 1954 with US-supplied Lockheed T-33As, of which the first six were delivered on 24 March that year. Towards the end of their operational careers, F-86 Sabres were added to the school, the last withdrawn from No 732 Sqn in 1973. Both Nos 731 and 732 Sqn then re-equipped with F-5Bs which had been briefly used by 21 Wing at Morón. The school was designated *Ala* 23 on 23 March 1987 and its squadrons became Nos 231 and 232.

TORREJON DE ARDOZ-MADRID

Location: Immediately N of Torrejón
ICAO code: LETO
Runway: 05/23 (13,400ft/4,087m)
Notable for having one of the longest runways in Europe, Torrejón has lost its USAF fighter wing but is still a busy base with several resident units. *Ala* 12 has half the EdA's EF-18 Hornet fleet in Nos 121 and 122 Sqn and the OCU, No 124 Sqn;

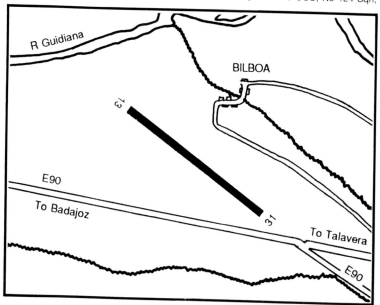

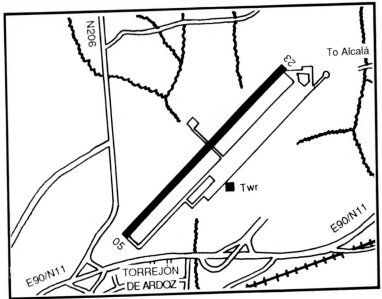

plus its last remaining Phantoms: the RF-4Cs of *Esc* 123. The VIP transport wing, *Ala* 45 moved from nearby Barajas airport in June 1992 with Boeing 707s (No 451 Sqn) and Falcon 20/5/900 and Navajo (No 452 Sqn). Water-bombing CL-215s belong to *Grupo* 43 (Nos 431 and 432 Sqn), whilst *Ala* 54 is the EdA's trials unit, with aircraft such as the Hornet, Aviocar and Tamiz. Remaining US facilities are operated by the 600th Air Base Group, but no aircraft are assigned. Spain's redundant F-4C Phantoms are stored on the airfield.

Ramps are on the east side of the runway and the nearest can be observed from the N206 near the 05 threshold. From a point one mile further north it is possible to walk the northern boundary and observe the northeast ramps with a telescope, but only in conditions of minimum heat haze.

Built following the Spanish-US defence agreement, Torrejón was assigned to SAC and became HQ of its 16th AF in July 1956. In addition to 'Reflex' B-47 Stratojet rotations, the base housed the escort fighters (F-86 Sabres, then F-102 Delta Daggers) of the 497th FIS. The F-102s passed to USAFE in July 1960 and returned to the US in June 1964, shortly

before 'Reflex' ended in March 1965. Torrejón and the 16th AF passed to USAFE in April 1966, with SAC's 98th Strat Wing as host for continued KC-135 rotations. On 27 April 1966, the 401st TFW transferred from England AFB with F-100D Super Sabres and later upgraded to F-4 Phantoms in 1970, then F-16 Fighting Falcons from December 1982. The 401st's last aircraft left the base in March 1992 and the wing (without aircraft) and HQ 16th AF moved to Aviano, Italy.

Spain's first resident fighter unit at Torrejón was *Ala* 6 which arrived from Getafe with its Sabres in May 1959 and became *Ala* 16 in 1965. The wing was the only one in the EdA to have Sabres optimised for air defence with fitments for AIM-9B Sidewinder AAMs. Deliveries of F-104G Starfighters for No 161 Sqn began on 5 March 1965 and after becoming (appropriately) No 104 Sqn in 1967 the wing handed back all 21 aircraft to the USA on 1 July 1972 after 20,000 loss-free hours. The Sabres were then ending their service lives, having flown with No 61, later No 102, later No 201 Sqn.

Shortly before, in March 1971, *Esc* 121 of the new *Ala* 12 had formed out of No 210 Sqn with ex-USAF F-4Cs, the first arriving in June, to be joined in May 1972 by No 122 Sqn. In support, three Boeing KC-97 Stratotankers were flown by No 123 Sqn until 1975. The F-4C force was stood down in March 1989 when Hornets began transferring from Zaragoza, and deliveries were completed in July 1990. An OCU, *Esc* 124, formed on 1 November 1992. Eight RF-4Cs were delivered to Torrejón on 11 January 1989 to augment four received in 1978 and equip newly-formed No 123 Sqn until well into the next century. *Grupo* 43 formed at Torrejón on 7 May 1980 to operate the CL-215s delivered since 1974 to the former No 404 Sqn.

VILLANUBLA-VALLADOLID

Location: 7½ miles (12km) NW of
  Valladolid
ICAO code: LEVD
Runway: 05/23 (9,843ft/3,000m)
Resident wing at this light transport base is *Ala* 37, which has Nos 371 and 372 Sqn equipped with CASA C.212 Aviocars.

From the civil terminal adjacent to Villanubla village the Aviocar ramp on the opposite side of the runway can be observed. The U-shaped detour in the N601 is unfenced and gives excellent views of the runway.

Villanubla was previously home to Spain's first indigenous jet trainer and attack aircraft, the Hispano Saeta. *Esc* 431 received the EdA's first HA 200A versions in 1963, followed by initial deliveries of the armed HA 200D in the following year. Expanded to include No 432 Sqn, the wing became *Grupo* 21 in 1967, comprising *Esc* 211 and 212 then was reduced to *Esc* 203 in 1971, on receipt of HA 220 Super Saetas. Jet operations ended in 1974 with disbandment of *Esc* 203 and the arrival from Albacete of *Ala* 37.

DHC-4 Caribous of No 372 Sqn waited until late in 1981 before No 371 was re-formed with ex-USAF C-7A versions of the aircraft. The Spanish Caribou fleet was concentrated at Villanubla from October 1985, but civilian sales began in the following year and the Caribou was finally withdrawn from EdA service on 12 June 1991. By then, 37 Wing had begun to receive Aviocars made surplus by delivery of CN.235s to 35 Wing at Getafe.

ZARAGOZA-VALENZUELA

Location: 7½ miles (12km) W of Zaragoza
ICAO code: LEZG (EdA); LEZA (USAF)
Runways: 12L/30R (9,842ft/3,000m);
  12R/30L (12,198ft/3,718m)
Once virtually a USAF base, Zaragoza is now home to one of Spain's two Hornet wings, *Grupo* 15 (Nos 151 and 152 Sqn)

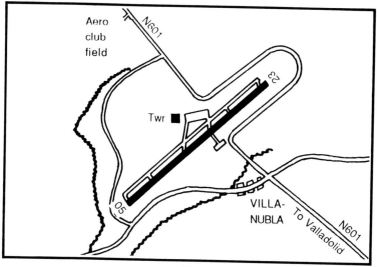

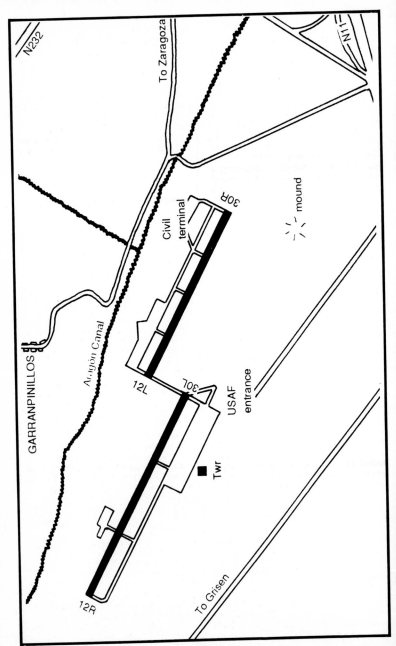

and its strategic transport wing, *Grupo* 31 (Nos 311 and 312 Sqn) of Hercules, comprising five KC-130H tankers, a 'stretched' C-130H-30 and the surviving six C-130Hs. The two Groups form *Ala* 31.

Scrubland surrounding the base makes circumnavigation possible in a cross-terrain vehicle, but should not be attempted in a saloon car. A mound is accessible from the road to the old USAF entrance and is a vantage point for early-morning (pre-heat haze) telescoping. From here, tracks head northeast under the 30R approach for photography. Beginning at the USAF entrance, the southern boundary can be traced to the 12R approach. On the opposite side it is possible to follow the north bank of the Aragón Canal, then cross southwards by bridge.

Vastly expanded following the Spanish-US defence treaty, Zaragoza became the first base to host SAC 'Reflex' B-47 Stratojet deployments in July 1957. These remained until May 1965, fighter escorts being the F-86 Sabres and F-102 Delta Daggers of the 431st FIS which returned to the US in May 1965. Passed to USAFE in April 1966, the base was held in reserve until 19 February 1970 when it became a weapons training site to replace that lost at Wheelus, Libya, after the 1969 coup.

The 7472nd Combat Support Group was reorganised as 406th Tac Fighter Training Group on 1 July 1970, becoming a Wing on 14 July 1972. US aircraft from throughout Europe regularly detached to Zaragoza to use the nearby Bardenas Reales range until the 1988 bases agreement with Spain specified an end to the regular US presence during 1991. SAC's lodger, the 34th Strategic Squadron, ended KC-135 and KC-10 detachments when the final tanker (a KC-10A) left the base on 9 January 1992. Occasional deployments are still permitted, however.

First Spanish jet aircraft at Zaragoza were the Sabres of *Ala* 2 (*Esc* 21), formed in 1956 and retitled 12 Wing (No 121 Sqn) in May 1965 shortly before disbanding. The jet refresher school, *Grupo* 41, was flying the EdA's last T-33As when its No 411 Sqn began converting to CASA Aviojets on 23 October 1981, followed by *Esc* 412. A six-ship team, the *Patruilla Amigo* formed in 1985 (predating the *Aguilas*), but the wing transferred to Matacán in July 1986. Spain's first Hercules were delivered early in 1974 to form

No 301 Sqn of *Grupo* 31 and as more were received, the unit was reorganised into Nos 311 and 312 Sqn in 1979, with No 312 taking the tankers.

In preparation for the Hornet, Spain's first hardened shelters (as distinct from US-built installations) were constructed at Zaragoza and a new wing, *Ala* 15, formed on 16 December 1985. Aircraft deliveries began on 10 July 1986, starting with two-seat EF-18Bs for pilot training. The wing was declared operational in December 1987 and became a Group in August 1989.

OTHER MILITARY AIR BASES:

- **Alcantarilla** 1¾ miles (3km) SW of Alcantarilla. *Escuela Militar de Paracaidismo/Esc* 721 (Aviocar).
- **Agoncillo** 6¾ miles (11km) E of Agoncillo (army). *Unidad de Helicopteros de Manoibra* III: *Sección Reconocimiento* (Bö105); *Compania Transporte Medio* (UH-1H).
- **Betéra** 12½ miles (20km) NW of Valancia (army). *Unidad de Helicopteros de Manoibra* II: *Sección Reconocimiento* (Bö105); *Compania Transporte Medio* (UH-1H).
- **Ciudad Real-Almagro** 13 miles (21km) SE of Ciudad Real (army). *Battalon de Helicopteros de Ataque* I: I *Compania HA* (Bö105); II *Compania HA* (Bö105).
- **Colmenar Viejo** (BA Coronel Maté/Los Remedios) 2½ miles (4km) N of Colmenar Viejo (army). *Jefatura de las FAMET* (UH-1, Cougar); *Unidad de Helicopteros de Transporte* V *Compania Transporte Medio* (UH-1H); *Compania Transporte Pesado* (Chinook); *Centro de Ensenanza de las FAMET* (Bö105, AB206, UH-1, OH-58).
- **El Copero** 5½ miles (9km) S of Seville (army). *Battalon de Helicopteros de Manoibra* IV *Sección Reconocimiento* (Bö105); *Compania Transporte Medio* (Cougar).
- **Cuatro Vientos-Madrid** 5 miles (8km) SW of Madrid. *Esc* 402 (Puma, Cougar); *Esc* 403 (Citation); *Esc* 803 (Aviocar; Cougar).
- **Gibraltar** (UK possession) adjacent to Spanish border. RAF staging post.
- **Granada-Armilla** 9¼ miles (15km) W of Granada. *Ala* 78/*Escuela de Helicopteros: Esc* 781 (Sikorsky S-76C); *Esc* 782 (Hughes 300C).

- **Jerez** 5½ miles (9km) NE of Jerez. *Ala 22: Esc* 221 and 222 (Orion, Aviocar) moving to Morón.
- **Matacan-Salamanca** 8¾ miles (14km) E of Salamanca. *Grupo de Escuelas Matacan: Grupo de Adiestramiento/Esc* 441 and 412 (Aviojet); *Grupo de Ensenanza/Esc* 744 and 745 (Aviocar).
- **Rota** 1¾ miles (3km) NE of Rota. (Spanish Navy:) *Escuadrilla* 003 (AB 212), 004 (Comanche, Twin Comanche, Citation), 005 (Sea King), 006 (Hughes 500M), 008 (AV-8A), 009 (AV-8B), 010 (SH-60B Seahawk); (US Navy:) VQ-2 (EP-3E-II Aries, P-3B Orion); detachments (KC-130, P-3C, C-9B).
- **San Javier-Murcia** 1¾ miles (3km) SSE of San Javier. *Academia del Aire: Esc* 791 (Tamiz, Bonanza); *Esc* 792 (Aviocar); *Esc* 793 (Aviojet); (sailplanes).
- **Tablada-Seville** 2½ miles (4km) SSW of Seville. Reserve.

Additionally: **Gando** (Canary Is) — *Ala* 46: *Esc* 461 (Aviocar), *Esc* 462 (Mirage F1), *Esc* 802 (Fokker 27MPA, Cougar); **Los Rodeos** (Tenerife) (army) — *Battalon de Helicopteros de Canarias VI (Sección Recco* — Bö105), *Compania Transporte Medio* (UH-1H); **Son San Juan** (Majorca) — *Esc* 801 (Aviocar, Cougar).

Suburban encroachment. *Esc* 402, the VIP helicopter transport unit equipped with Pumas and (illustrated) Cougars, is based at Cuatro Vientos in the suburbs of Madrid, where blocks of flats overlook the ramp. *AGPPA*

Getafe (Madrid) is the home base of *Ala* 35, one of whose CN.235s — actually the first of two VIP T.19C variants — is here awaiting the first sortie of the day. *AGPPA*

SWITZERLAND

Switzerland's *Flugwaffe* (Air Force) is a branch of the army (*Flugwaffenbrigade* 31) with an unusual organisation directly relevant to the history of airfield development in this long-time neutral state. The Swiss take their neutrality seriously and have large and well-trained reservist forces which can be mobilised at short notice. Accordingly, the *Flugwaffe* order of battle is entirely transformed in the event of war.

Peacetime duties comprise the usual airspace policing and light transport role, plus a sizeable training commitment. These are undertaken from prominent, well-known airfields by six combat squadrons (comprising the *Uberwachungsgeschwader* — Surveillance Wing), four schools and three miscellaneous units, backed by elements of the eight wartime light transport (mostly helicopter) squadrons. Requirements of training are such that detachments of many units will invariably be found at bases other than their own — each airfield has the appearance of a miniature Swiss Air Force.

In wartime, the full-time and reservist elements would move to their combat stations, abandoning those peacetime bases not equipped with hardened facilities. Switzerland has a network of war airfields, sometimes using roads as runways, the aircraft accommodation for which is underground, often in mountain caves.

The visitor will occasionally chance upon a training exercise under way at one of these bases, but the aircraft are normally kept at the peacetime stations. Very little is known of the underground facilities and about the only photograph officially released shows aircraft hung from the roof of an underground cavern to save storage space. To reach their hangars, aircraft taxi past steel doors into the caves or — allegedly — are taken down in lifts. At Sion, however, overground shelters have been constructed for F-18 Hornets in the style of U-boat pens.

Switzerland is Europe's aircraft carrier. Where most countries' military aviation is undertaken at bases which can be frustratingly large for the enthusiast, geography makes Swiss valley-floor airfields as cramped as the deck of a carrier. Almost all offer excellent views of flying with the added benefit of interesting backgrounds. The main bases usually have a *spotter-splatz* lay-by.

By the end of 1994, the last *Flugwaffe* Hunters will have been retired from the reserve squadrons, leaving the Mirage III and F-5E Tiger II as the front-line equipment. On order for delivery from 1997 are 34 Hornets which will equip three squadrons. Training is undertaken by Pilatus PC-7s and BAe Hawks, whilst a couple of LearJets provide VIP transport and

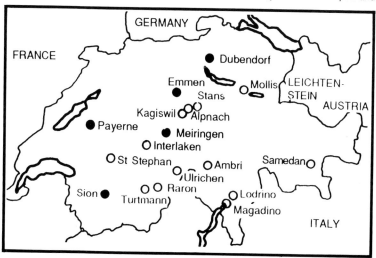

medical evacuation. The light transport squadrons (*Leichtetransportstaffeln*) are numbered 1-8, of which No 7 has Turbo Porters and the remainder fly either the Alouette II and III or Alouette IIIs and Cougars.

Badges indicating the operating unit were extremely rare, but are now seen more often. The complete cross-reference below includes units which have disbanded or which carry no markings. Until they were leaked a few years ago, operating locations for reservist squadrons were a closely-guarded secret. It has, therefore, been impossible to compile comprehensive airfield histories including unit re-equipment dates. As an indication of recent history, the jet types previously and currently flown by squadrons are included with the badge information here-under.

Combat squadrons:
- No 1 Stylised eagle, side view (Hunter, Tiger)
- No 2 A heron, one leg raised (Venom, Hunter disbanded 6 May 1993)
- No 3 A bulldog's head (Venom, Hunter, Mirage)
- No 4 Witch on broomstick, upon a four-leaf clover (Hunter, Mirage)
- No 5 Wildcat's face (Hunter, to disband)
- No 6 Cartoon Swiss Guard (Venom, Tiger)
- No 7 Leaping fish (Hunter, to disband)
- No 8 Cartoon swordfish (Hunter, Tiger)
- No 9 Stylised witch on broomstick (Venom; disbanded)
- No 10 Stylised eagle's head (Venom, Mirage)
- No 11 Tiger's face (Hunter, Tiger)
- No 12 Winged halberd (Venom, Vampire; now PC-9)
- No 13 Stylised butterfly (Venom, Tiger)
- No 14 Two penguins (Venom; now various)
- No 15 Paper aircraft (Venom, Hunter, to disband)
- No 16 A dragon (Mirage)
- No 17 Stylised eagle diving (Mirage)
- No 18 A jaguar (Hunter, Tiger)
- No 19 Stylised stork (Hunter, Tiger)
- No 20 A buffalo (Venom, Hunter, to disband)
- No 21 A cat riding a shark (Hunter, to disband)

Light support squadrons:
- No 1 A bat
- No 2 A dragonfly in plan view
- No 3 Stylised helicopter over mountains
- No 4 Helicopter in the shape of '4'
- No 5 A grasshopper
- No 6 Stylised dragonfly, head-on
- No 7 Cartoon animal beneath a parachute

Switzerland's major military flying display was the annual *Flugmeisterschaft* competition between fighter units, held at Dubendorf. The last was in 1991, but from the following year, Dubendorf, Emmen and Payerne have had one or more 'visiting days' (*Militärflugzeug Besichtingstage*) per year for the public. Normally either a morning or afternoon event, these are not air displays in the accepted sense.

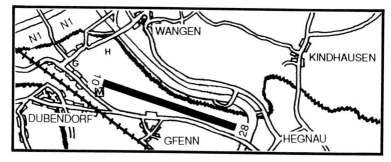

DUBENDORF

Location: 5 miles (8km) NE of Zurich
Runway: 10/28

Squadrons resident at Dubendorf in peacetime are No 10 with Mirage IIIRS tactical reconnaissance aircraft and No 18 in the interceptor role with F-5E Tigers. Additionally, Dubendorf and Payerne are the two main bases of *Instrumentation Fliegerstaffel* 14, which checks pilots on their instrument flying skills, borrowing aircraft as required. The base is not intended to war operations.

Typical aircraft which might be seen at Dubendorf include the Mirage IIIRS, F-5E, PC-6 Turbo Porter, PC-7 Turbo Trainer, PC-9, Cougar and Alouette II/III. There is an official spotters' lay-by on the southern perimeter road immediately north of Gfenn and the well-stocked air force museum is marked 'M' on the map. Northwest of the museum is the overhaul hangar with thoughtfully-provided windows in the rear. Continuing clockwise, the visitor can leave by the main gate,

pass the rear of more hangars on the northwest perimeter and park in a cul-de-sac by the helicopter hangar (H). From here a footpath runs along the river bank to the Mirage hangar on the north side, opposite the museum.

EMMEN

Location: 2½ miles (4km) NE of Luzern
Runway: 04/22

Emmen is the peacetime base of the BAe Hawk advanced trainers flown by *Pilotenschule* 55, comprising half of *Fliegerschule II Teil* (Flying School, Stage 2). It is not a wartime station.

Aircraft seen routinely at Emmen also include Hunters (until late 1994), F-5Es, Pilatus P-3s, PC-7s, Turbo Porters and Alouettes. The F&W aircraft works is on the east side of the runway, by highway 26. The minor road running parallel to the runway on its west side has an official spotters' lay-by abeam the 22 threshold.

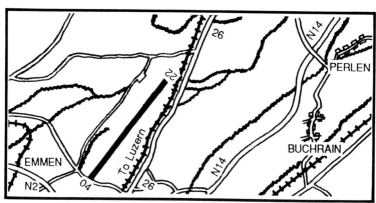

Going down? A No 11 Sqn F-5E Tiger II is prepared for towing inside the pens at Payerne. An unconfirmed report suggests that these include a lift to an underground hangar. *Mike Bursell*

Minus the Mirage III, this view of Payerne could be a film set for *The Sound of Music*. Swiss bases provide ample opportunity for interesting backgrounds. *AGPPA*

Locally-assembled Alouette IIIs are to be found in service with seven light support squadrons. *Paul Jackson*

Vanishing sight: the last Swiss Hunters are being withdrawn during 1994. Steep ground rises behind the Pilatus overhaul works at Stans. *Paul Jackson*

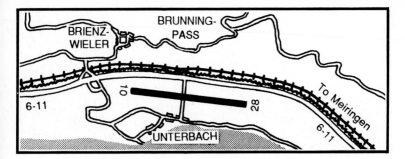

South of this are Hawk, Hunter and F-5E hangars and ramps on *both* sides of the road. A public road with traffic-lights control passes through the 04 threshold.

Hangars and ramps are on the southeast side of the runway, from where taxiways lead to hillside caverns. A small hangar for Pilatus P-3s is just north of Unterbach.

MEIRINGEN
Location: 3 miles (5km) NW of Meiringen
Runway: 10/28
Ground-attack F-5E Tigers of *Fliegerstaffel* 11 are the only peacetime residents at Meiringen. In wartime, this squadron would move to Alpnach and the base would accept two reservist air defence squadrons of Tigers: No 8 (also with an attack commitment) and No 13.

Visitors to Meiringen may also see Hunters in temporary residence until the end of 1994. When approaching from the north, a high-level view of the airfield can be obtained from the Brunningpass.

PAYERNE
Location: 1 mile (2km) NW of Payerne
Runway: 05/23

This major base hosts three squadrons of the *Uberwachungsgeschwader* for peacetime operations. *FlgStf* 1 has Tigers for reconnaissance and attack duties; and Nos 16 and 17 are Switzerland's two longest-serving air defence squadrons, both equipped with the Mirage IIIS. There is also in residence part of *IFlgStf* 14, the instrument rating squadron with loaned aircraft. Nos 1 and 16 would leave in wartime to be replaced by air defence

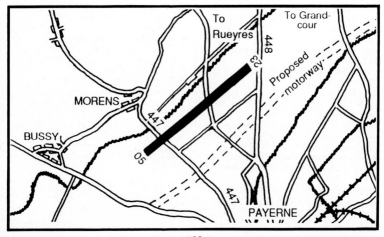

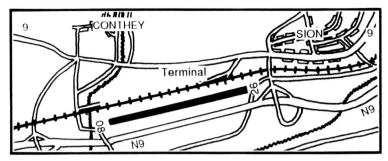

Tigers of *FlgStf* 18 and four Mirage IIIRS recce aircraft of No 4 Sqn.

Aircraft types regularly seen at Payerne comprise the Mirage IIIS, Tiger, Hunter (1994 only), P-3, Turbo Trainer, PC-9 and Alouette III. There is an official spotters' lay-by on the north side of the runway, close to the control tower. Hangars are spread throughout the airfield and good views can be obtained from many vantage points. Two roads crossing the runway are controlled by traffic lights.

SION

Location: 1 mile (2km) SW of Sion
ICAO code: LSGS
Runway: 08/26 (6,562ft/2,000m)

A peacetime training base and civil airport, Sion normally accommodates half of the Hawk fleet, serving with *Pilotenschule 255*. Together with the aircraft at Emmen, the Hawks constitute *Fliegerschule II Teil*. Also resident is part of *Zeilfliegerstaffel* 12 and its target-towing PC 9s. Sion's wartime role is reconnaissance with the Tiger IIs of No 6 Sqn and Mirage IIIRSs of No 3 Sqn.

In addition to the above resident aircraft, Turbo Trainers and Alouettes will often be seen at Sion. The civil terminal gives a good view of the military ramps and hangars on the south side of the runway. Farner's overhaul hangar is in the southeast corner, with the main air force complex — including new hangars for the Hawks — in the centre. To the southwest are new hardened shelters for Hornets.

OTHER MILITARY AIR BASES:

● **Alpnach** 3 miles (5km) NNE of Sarnen. Wartime only. *FlgStf* 11 and 19 (Tiger II).

● **Ambri** 4¼ miles (7km) SE of Airolo. Wartime only. No known assigned units.
● **Interlaken** Peacetime training base (various). Wartime base of *FlgStf* 7 (Hunter — until 1994) and *FlgStf* 24 (det) (Hunter T68/ECM).
● **Kagiswil** ½ mile (1km) N of Sarnen. Light transport training (Alouette, Cougar).
● **Lodrino** 12½ miles (20km) NW of Locarno. Light transport training (Alouette, Cougar).
● **Magadino** 3¾ miles (6km) ESE of Locarno. *Fliegerschule I Teil* (*Pilotenrekrutenschulen* 42 and 242) (P-3, Turbo Trainer).
● **Mollis** ½ mile (1km) SE of Näfels. Wartime only. *FlgStf* 20 (Hunter — until 1994).
● **Raron** 12 miles (20km) E of Sierre. Wartime only. *Escadrille d'Aviation* 5 (Hunter — until 1994).
● **Samedan** 2½ miles (4km) SE of Sankt Moritz. Peacetime base for *ZFlgStf* 12 (det) (PC-9).
● **St Stephan** 2½ miles (4km) S of Zweisimmen. Wartime only. *FlgStf* 15 (Hunter — until 1994); *FlgStf* 24 (det) (Hunter T68/ECM).
● **Stans** ½ mile (1km) SW of Buochs. Peacetime training base (various) and Pilatus factory. Wartime base of *FlgStf* 10 (Mirage IIIRS); *FlgStf* 16 (Mirage IIIS).
● **Turtmann** 7½ miles (12km) E of Sierre. Wartime only. *Escadrille d'Aviation* 1 (Tiger); *FlgStf* 21 (Hunter — until 1994).
● **Ulrichen** Closed 1993 (former wartime base).

Also, second-class war bases at Frutlingen, Reichenbach, Saanen, Sanvittore and Zweisimmen.

APPENDIX

THE NEXT STEP

To assist those travelling one step beyond the geographical borders of this book's main section, brief details follow of military air bases in Italy, Norway and Sweden.

Inclusion of the two northern states provides an opportunity to remind readers of the differing attitudes to aviation enthusiasts around Europe. Norway, although a NATO member, is less tolerant than many of its compatriots and even frowns upon applications for supervised visits to stations. Neutral Sweden has similar attitudes, limiting the opportunities for unhindered spotting to the few air shows held in each country.

In Italy, strict laws prevent photography near aerodromes. That said, the authorities apply the same level of enforcement to this statute as is afforded to many other regulations in that country. In short, the rules vary from base to base.

ITALY

- **Amendola** 9¼ miles (15km) NE of Foggia. 32º *Stormo*/13º *Gruppo* (G.91Y), 201º & 204º *Gruppi* (G.91T).
- **Aviano** 2½ miles (4km) S of Aviano. USAF: 31st FW/510th & 555th FS (F-16C) forming 1994.
- **Bari-Palese** 5 miles (8km) NW of Bari. 512º *Squadriglia* (various, on loan)
- **Bolzano** 2½ miles (4km) S of Bolzano. Army: 24º *Gruppo* (SM.1019, AB.206), 54º *Gruppo* (AB.205), 34º *Gruppo* (detached to Venaria; AB.205, AB.206), 44º *Gruppo* (detached to Aosta; AB.205, AB.206).
- **Bresso** Immediately W of Bresso. Army: 53º *Gruppo* (AB.205, AB.206).
- **Brindisi** Immediately N of Brindisi. 14º *Stormo*/84º *Centro* (HH-3F).
- **Cagliari-Elmas** 3 miles (5km) W of Cagliari, Sardinia. 30º *Stormo*/86º *Gruppo* (Atlantic); Army: 21º *Gruppo* (AB.205, AB.206, SM.1019).
- **Cameri/Novara** 6¼ miles (10km) NNE of Cameri. 53º *Stormo*/21º *Gruppo* (F-104S/ASA).
- **Casarsa** 1 mile (2km) W of Casarsa. Army: 49º *Gruppo* (A.129, AB.412, A.109).
- **Catania-Fontanarossa** Immediately SW of Catania, Sicily. Navy: 2º & 3º

Grupelicot (AB.212 & Sea King); Army: 30º *Gruppo* (A.109, AB.212, SM.1019).
- **Cervia** 3¾ miles (6km) SW of Cervia. 8º *Stormo*/23º *Gruppo* (F-104S/ASA), 101º *Gruppo* (G.91Y).
- **Ciampino** Immediately SW of Ciampino. 15º *Stormo*/46º *Centro* (AB.212), 85º *Gruppo* (HH-3F, AB.212); 31º *Stormo*/93º *Gruppo* (PD-808, AS-61TS, Falcon 50), 306º *Gruppo* (PD-808, DC-9, Gulfstream III).
- **Decimomannu** 12½ miles (20km) NW of Cagliari, Sardinia. 670º *Squadriglia* (AB.212); NATO weapons training base.
- **Firenza-Peretola** Immediately N of Firenza (Florence). Army: 27º *Gruppo* (AB.206, SM.1019).
- **Frosinone** 3 miles (5km) W of Frosinone. 208º *Gruppo* (MDH 500, AB.212)
- **Ghedi** 4¼ miles (7km) E of Bagnolo Mella. 6º *Stormo*/102º (F-104S/ASA), 154º *Gruppo* (Tornado).
- **Gioia del Colle** 2 miles (3km) S of Gioia. 36º *Stormo*/12º *Gruppo* (F-104S/ASA), 156º *Gruppo* (Tornado).
- **Grazzanise** 3 miles (5km) SW of Grazzanise. 9º *Stormo*/10º *Gruppo* (F-104S/ASA).
- **Grosseto** Immediately W of Grosetto. 4º *Stormo*/9º *Gruppo* (F-104S/ASA), 20º *Gruppo* (TF-104G, F-104S/ASA).
- **Grottaglie** 1 mile (2km) SW of Grottaglie. Navy: 4º *Grupelicot* (AB.212AS); *Grupo Embarcada* (T/AV-8B).
- **Guidonia** Immediately SE of Guidonia. 303º *Gruppo* (Avanti, P.166-DL3, S.208); 432º *Squadriglia* (S.208 & sailplanes).
- **Latina** 5½ miles (9km) N of Latina. 207º *Gruppo* (P.166, SF.260).
- **Lecce-Galatina** 5 miles (8km) NNW of Lecce. 61º *Brigata*/212º & 213º *Gruppi* (MB.339).
- **Luni-Sarzana** 2 miles (3km) SE of Sarzana. Navy: 1º & 5º *Grupelicot* (Sea King & AB.212AS).
- **Padova** SW outskirts of Padova (Padua). Army: 55º *Gruppo* (AB.205).
- **Piacenza** 2½ miles (4km) E of Vigolzone. 50º *Stormo*/155º *Gruppo* (Tornado).
- **Pisa-San Guisto** Immediately S of Pisa. 46º *Brigata*/2º & 98º *Gruppi* (G.222), 50º *Gruppo* (Hercules); Army: 26º *Gruppo* (AB.206, AB.212).

- **Pratica-di-Mare** 9¼ miles (15km) SE of Lido di Astia. 14º *Stormo*/8º *Gruppo* (PD-808VIP/TP/RM, G.222RM, B 707TT), 71º *Gruppo* (PD-808GE, G.222VS); 311º *Gruppo* (flight-trials).
- **Rimini-Maramar** 3 miles (5km) SE of Rimini. 14º *Stormo*/83º *Centro* (HH-3F).
- **Salerno-Pontecagno** 2½ miles (4km) SE of Pontecagno. Army: 20º *Gruppo* (AB.206, AB.412, SM.1019).
- **Sigonella** 6¼ miles (10km) SW of Catania, Sicily. 41º *Stormo*/88º *Gruppo* (Atlantic); US Navy detachments.
- **Trapani-Birgi** 5 miles (8km) S of Trapani, Sicily. 15º *Stormo*/82º *Centro* (HH-3F); 37º *Stormo*/18º *Gruppo* (F-104S/ASA); NATO/RAF detachment (E-3 Sentry).
- **Treviso-Istrana** 7½ miles (12km) WNW of Treviso. 2º *Stormo*/14º *Gruppo* (AMX); 51º *Stormo*/22º *Gruppo* (AMX).
- **Udine-Rivolto** 10½ miles (17km) SW of Udine. 313º *Gruppo 'Frecce Tricolori'* (MB.339); Army: 25º *Gruppo* (AB.205, AB.206).
- **Urbe** N outskirts of Rome. Army: 28º *Gruppo* (AB.206, SM.1019).
- **Vercelli** 2 miles (3km) S of Vercelli. Army: 23º *Gruppo* (AB.205, AB.206).
- **Villafranca-Verona** 6¼ miles (10km) SW of Verona. 3º *Stormo*/28º & 132º *Gruppi* (AMX).
- **Viterbo** 2½ miles (4km) W of Viterbo. Army: 11º & 12º *Gruppi* (Chinook), 51º *Gruppo* (AB.205, AB.412); *Centro ALE* (all army types, including Dornier 228).

Norway
- **Andøya** Immediately SE of Andennes. *Skv* 333 (Orion).
- **Bardufoss** Immediately NE of Bardufoss. *Skv* 337 (Lynx); *Skv* 339 (AB.412).
- **Bodø** Immediately SW of Bodø. *Skv* 330 (Sea King); *Skv* 331 & 334 (F-16A); *Skv* 719 (Twin Otter).
- **Gardermoen** 5 miles (8km) NW of Jessheim. *Skv* 335 (Hercules, Falcon 20).
- **Ørland** Adjacent to Brekstad. *Skv* 338 (F-16A); NATO/RAF detachment (E-3 Sentry)
- **Rygge** 5 miles (8km) SE of Moss. *Skv* 332 & 336 (F-16A); *Skv* 720 (AB.412).
- **Vårnes** 7½ miles (12km) E of Trondheim. Flying School (MFI-15).

Sweden
- **Angelhölm** 3 miles (5km) N of Angelhölm. F10 (J 35/Sk 35 Draken, SF/SH/AJ 37 Viggen, Bell 204, Saab 105).
- **Berga** 3¾ miles (6km) N of Högsby. Navy: 11 *HkpDiv* (KV-107, AB.206, Aviocar).
- **Boden** Immediately S of Boden. Army: AF1 (AB.204, AB.206, AB.412, Bö105).
- **Göteborg-Säve** 5½ miles (9km) NW of Göteborg (Gothenburg). Navy: 13 *HkpDiv* (KV-107, AB.206).
- **Karlsborg** Immediately S of Karlsborg. F6 (AJ 37 Viggen, Bell 204, Bö105, Saab 105).
- **Linköping-Malmslatt** Immediately W of Linköping. *Malfkygdivisionen* (Lansen, Caravelle, Sabreliner); Army AF2 (Hughes 300, Bö105). Army: *Arméflyskolan* (all types)
- **Ljungbyhed** Immediately NW of Ljungbyhet. F5 (Saab 105, Bulldog).
- **Luleå-Kallax** 3 miles (5km) S of Luleå. F21 (SF/SH/JA 37 Viggen, Bell 204, Super Puma, Saab 105, King Air).
- **Ostersund-Frösön** 3 miles (5km) NW of Frösön. F4 (JA 37 Viggen, Bell 204, Saab 105).
- **Ronneby** 2 miles (3km) NNW of Kallinge. F17 (JA/SF/SH 37 Viggen, Super Puma, Saab 105, King Air); Navy: 12 *HkpDiv* (KV-107, AB.206).
- **Såtenäs** Immediately W of Såtenäs. F7 (Gripen, AJ 37 Viggen, Hercules, Bö105, Saab 105, King Air).
- **Söderhamn** 3 miles (5km) ESE of Söderhamn. F15 (AJ 37 Viggen, Super Puma, Saab 105).
- **Uppsala** 3 miles (5km) NNW of Uppsala. F16 (JA 37 Viggen, Saab 105, Bell 204, Saab 340).